DATE DUE

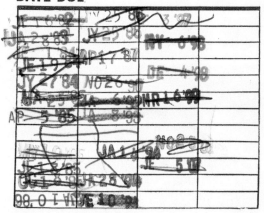

RIVERSIDE CITY COLLEGE
LIBRARY
Riverside, California

DE '81

DEMCO

Grandfather Rock

GRANDFATHER ROCK

The New Poetry and the Old

DELACORTE PRESS
NEW YORK

DAVID MORSE

This book is for Ginny

CONTENTS

The New Poetry and the Old   1

Ancient Voices   9

Tales of Brave Ulysses,
   ERIC CLAPTON AND MARTIN SHARP   11
The Sirens' Song, HOMER   13

Story of Isaac, LEONARD COHEN   16
The Parable of the Old Men and the Young,
   WILFRED OWEN   18

From the Underworld, HOWARD BLAIKLEY   20
Orpheus and Eurydice, OVID   21

Loneliness and Love   27

Four and Twenty, STEPHEN STILLS   30
To the Reader, CHARLES BAUDELAIRE   30

Suzanne, LEONARD COHEN   33
Dover Beach, MATTHEW ARNOLD   35

Albatross, JUDY COLLINS   37
Patterns, AMY LOWELL   39

In My Life,
   JOHN LENNON AND PAUL MC CARTNEY   43
The Old Familiar Faces, CHARLES LAMB   43

Death   47

Casey Jones, ROBERT HUNTER   52
Joseph Mica, ANONYMOUS   53

Bishop Cody's Last Request, TOM PAXTON   55
The Bishop Orders His Tomb at Saint Praxed's
   Church, ROBERT BROWNING   57

Tigers of Wrath   65

Masters of War, BOB DYLAN   68
England in 1819, PERCY BYSSHE SHELLEY   70

The Fool on the Hill,
   JOHN LENNON AND PAUL MC CARTNEY   72
The Dawn, WILLIAM BUTLER YEATS   73

The Continuing Story of Bungalow Bill,
   JOHN LENNON AND PAUL MC CARTNEY   75
buffalo bill's, e.e cummings   76

Pictures of a City, ROBERT FRIPP AND PETER SINFIELD   78
London, WILLIAM BLAKE   78

The Observation, DONOVAN LEITCH   80
Ye Hasten to the Grave! PERCY BYSSHE SHELLEY   80

Prophetic Voices   83

Bad Moon Rising, JOHN FOGERTY   85
A Dirge, PERCY BYSSHE SHELLEY   86

Stories of the Street, LEONARD COHEN   88
The Second Coming, WILLIAM BUTLER YEATS   89

The King Must Die, BERNIE TAUPIN   91
The Death of Kings, WILLIAM SHAKESPEARE   93

Anthems of the New Republic   97

Father of Night, BOB DYLAN   100
Song of Myself (22), WALT WHITMAN   101

Woodstock, JONI MITCHELL   102
To the Garden the World, WALT WHITMAN   103

We Can Be Together, PAUL KANTNER   105
Song of Myself (24), WALT WHITMAN   106

Wooden Ships,
   DAVID CROSBY, PAUL KANTNER, STEPHEN STILLS   108
Asia's Song, PERCY BYSSHE SHELLEY   110

New Morning, BOB DYLAN   112
Song, ROBERT BROWNING   113

Spaces   117

Dawn Is a Feeling, MIKE PINDER   117
The Dream (Part 1), LORD BYRON   118

Chelsea Morning, JONI MITCHELL   119
The Morning Watch, HENRY VAUGHAN   120

Cactus Tree, JONI MITCHELL   121

Unthrifty Loveliness (Sonnet IV),
    WILLIAM SHAKESPEARE   123

Gypsy Eyes, JIMI HENDRIX   124

Sweet-and-Twenty, WILLIAM SHAKESPEARE   125

I Think I Understand, JONI MITCHELL   126

Our Journey Had Advanced, EMILY DICKINSON   127

Strawberry Fields Forever,
    JOHN LENNON AND PAUL MC CARTNEY   127

The Lotus Eaters (Choric Songs 3 and 4),
    ALFRED, LORD TENNYSON   129

She Wandered Through the Garden Fence,
    KEITH REID   130

The Mental Traveller, WILLIAM BLAKE   131

Final Notes   137

Index of Titles, Authors and Performers   139

Index of First Lines   143

ACKNOWLEDGMENTS

Thanks are due the following for special generosity in making work available for this book: Lynn Music Limited for "From the Underworld," Ice Nine Publishing Co. for "Casey Jones," Jondora Music for "Bad Moon Rising," and The Belknap Press of Harvard University Press and the Trustees of Amherst College for "Our Journey Had Advanced"; and for help with information and materials, Bernard Stollman at ESP Records, Bruce Harris at Elektra and Alan Rosenberg at Reprise, and the people at *Rolling Stone*.

Special thanks are due Pat Mancini. Without her help the book might never have gotten started.

For adding their bit to the flow of ideas, and for general encouragement, thanks to Bob Parsons, Dennis Dermody, Jack Quigley, Arthur Daigon, Dan Rubin, Kevin Fisher, Peter Bellis, Hugh Gerechter, and my father and mother.

Thanks to all the good folk at Delacorte Press, and especially Debby Baker, not only for her editorial assistance but also for bringing homebaked bread and good cheer.

Thanks to my wife for her patience and durable wit.

Grandfather Rock

THE NEW POETRY AND THE OLD

Here are rock lyrics and traditional poems from across a span of three thousand years. In a few cases we can see a direct influence; in others it's a matter of old and new addressing themselves to the same ideas and emotions. But in all cases they speak to each other.

As long as we have found the technology and patience to listen to dolphins and astronauts mouthing commonplaces across the wastes, why not listen to each other, to the skein of human words stretching across the millennia? Enjoy the new and old sounds together, and test the relevance of both.

You might think of this book as an open-ended framework of print with an acoustic effect. It should be approached with albums in hand. To read the lyrics without ever hearing the music is to miss most of the beauty and force of rock. To read the poetry with your eyes alone is to rob it, too, of a part of its voice.

All poetry is first sound. Homer may have been a blind street singer or a group, but the homeric verses were spoken and sung long before they were scratched onto parchment. The great epics of England and France—*Beowulf* and *Chanson de Roland*—were sung. Chaucer was a great talker, a keeper of a customs house with a ready place by the fireside for travelers to tell their tales. Blind

Milton composed some of the greatest lines in English poetry by ear alone. Wordsworth composed the whole of "Tintern Abbey" while traveling from Tintern to Bristol, without ever setting pen to paper.

When we imprison Chaucer and Shakespeare in books we sometimes forget their claim to the ear.

Our eyes anesthetize.

One of the things rock and roll has done recently is to open our ears again. And, in opening our ears, it has awakened us to the other senses that were a rich complement of the oral tradition.

Elizabethan drama, newly descended from religious pageants, was performed in theaters roiling with the scent of lantern smoke and people and wine and oranges, the clash of brass-beaten alarums and stench of gunpowder, the laughter and catcalls and pelting of actors with bad fruit, the occasional riots, the cheers mingled with the cries of beer vendors and hustlers. The excitement of a new play was felt in the palace and in the streets.

Think of those fine white marble statues of ancient Greece we admire within the hush of museums, how the Greeks originally painted them with colors of bright blue and apricot and decorated them with garlands of flowers, attending them with votive offerings, wine and noisy celebrations. Now rock restores sensuality to the literary milieu.

Immediacy. Magic. Sensuality. Celebration. All were part of the oral tradition which we lost, not with the advent of books, as McLuhan would have us believe, but with industrial rationalization. A calculated efficiency that insures us against the accident of fun, and sells us snowmmobiles instead.

"The Fool on the Hill," by Lennon and McCartney, sounds a protest in the spirit of Yeats' "The Dawn," not against literacy but against sterility, against a mode of life which has become literally *senseless.*

Rock restores sensation by returning us to the oral tradition. Although musical purists may sometimes disparage lyrics and partisans may defend good old rock 'n' roll against the inroads of literacy, the root sound of rock is a human voice. Chuck Berry. Little Richard. It may be the voice of the blues or it may go back to Homer or Blake. Or it may belong unequivocally to the present, as some of Frank Zappa's sounds do. But the great themes of literature are present in rock—love, death, beauty, loneliness, despair, faith; even some of those stirrings of the human heart for which there are no names. And even the most zapped-out electronic fortissimo has its origin somewhere on this human scale.

Is rock poetry? People still ask.

Instead they should listen to "Suzanne" and "Like a Rolling Stone," "Eleanor Rigby," "The End," and "Chelsea Morning." These are beautiful songs, and beautiful poetry, however you judge them.

We are in the process of a social revolution—a vast shift in our modes of thinking, our values, our institutions, our responses to people—a revolution too huge to be the property of political faction or leader, too much the property of the many to be articu-. lated by the few.

Rock is the poetry of that revolution. So is much of the best poetry of the last two centuries. Blake and Shelley were outraged at war, struggled against the weight of outworn creeds and dehumanizing institutions, against the denial of the senses; Matthew Arnold despaired at the human scale being inundated by the rising tide of technology; Whitman was exuberant with the different specter of a vast human love.

Poetry is the rock and roll of the past. It is the only way to meet certain people with really beautiful minds.

Everybody who has attended his share of rock festivals has had, probably at least once, something on the order of a religious experience. For Tom Paxton it might have been the 1969 Isle of Wight concert, where he received an unexpectedly huge ovation. "This is the happiest day of my life," Paxton choked. It was a beatific cliché, because it was said with utter sincerity, because it was as false as it was true, and because the audience understood it that way and not as showbiz. Tom Paxton might have said that at that particular instant he felt he was *God;* and the audience was *God.* This was an audience that had come to see Dylan. So it was also a way of cutting through the hype that was turning Dylan into an Event, of the crowd refusing to be manipulated by the concert producers and saying that at this particular instant *this* was the performance that was beautiful.

Mysticism, yes. But a poetic moment. And the incident points to two characteristics of the new culture—a mysticism amounting to an actual religiosity, and a stubborn refusal to accept a bill of fare handed down by critical authority. Neither is foolproof; mysticism can go astray and crowds can be hyped. But this particular combination of religiosity and an insistence on responding to a performance on its own merits is surely what animated audiences at the inception of the great periods of the performing arts, when the Bacchanal celebrations were being turned into theater by experimenters like Sophocles and Aristophanes, who vied with each other for fame and reputation; and again in the theaters of Elizabethan England.

Bath, Wiltshire, 1970

Dusk and a chill wind blowing from the north, across the Salisbury Plain. Everybody hunkered into their ponchos and against each other for warmth, settling in for Pink Floyd. Everywhere the glowing tips of joss sticks and weed and scattered larger glows of bonfires at the edges of the crowd. Smoke drifting across the 250,000 people, blanketing the hollows with blue translucency.

The stage is pulsing now with soft lavender explosions and the ethereal sounds of Pink Floyd. I resist its pull, picking my way toward the north edge of the crowd, stepping over bedrolls, binoculars and yogurt cups, hands and faces, past marker sticks tied with Day-Glo streamers, one sole cabbage, wilting, and empty bleach bottles thumping in the wind. Threading my way at last to the outskirts, past wisping campfires and tents, between trucks parked in the mud, and following the fence up the hill, I stop at the top of the second slope and look back.

The crowd sprawls across the hillside, becoming a blue haze. The surrounding hills are dark. To the north somewhere is Stonehenge. Stars are twinkling. The stage glows magenta, appearing larger because of the giant screens on either side, confusing one's sense of scale, and pulsing with the unearthly science fiction sound of Pink Floyd; color dapples rotating, fluid projections squashing diaphanously amidst pop-on slides, and from the front of the stage a column of smoke rising, undulating violet and red.

The scale shifts eerily. Here are a quarter of a million people assembled on the Salisbury Plain around what suddenly can only be a gargantuan campfire. A sense of the globe curving away into darkness. The sense of something glacial, of being a disembodied spectator to one of those vast migrations that accompanied the ice ages. An electronic bonfire. Duplicatable: all over the planet, a gathering of tribes.

I shivered.

Words struggle now, to convey the grandeur of the scene and the scope of sensations within—fear, as though an impulse older than I could understand had touched an ancient sorrow into newness. Words struggle, always in danger of dislocating the fragile membrane which may appear for an instant to connect the individual with the primal body of man. Tom Paxton struggling to express a communion for which there is no liturgy. Matthew Arnold struggling to express the loss of God.

Poetry. Rock. They become the same.

Ancient Voices

SOMETIMES when a contemporary artist has built on a visibly ancient foundation, we have to ask, *Is it for real?* Is the artist simply exploiting a hallowed theme, or has he made it his own?

If we have to ask, the question is probably legitimate. But in some cases the material has been transformed so magically into a thing which is as new as it is old that we don't even think to ask.

Here is such a song.

If you need proof that Homer is alive today, just listen to Clapton and Sharp's "Tales of Brave Ulysses."

"Tales of Brave Ulysses," by Eric Clapton and Martin Sharp, recorded by Cream on *Disraeli Gears*, 1967
"The Sirens' Song," from Book XII of *The Odyssey*, by Homer, ca. 700 B.C., translated by Robert Fitzgerald

---

Ulysses had fought at Troy for ten years. He was eager to get home by the time he approached the deadly Sirens, and Circe's advice had made it clear what happened to anyone who heard their song:

The Sêirenês will sing his mind away
on their sweet meadow lolling. There are bones
of dead men rotting in a pile beside them
and flayed skins shrivel around the spot.
　　Steer wide;
keep well to seaward; plug your oarsmen's ears
with beeswax kneaded soft; none of the rest
should hear that song.
　　But if you wish to listen,
let the men tie you in the lugger, hand
and foot, back to the mast, lashed to the mast,
so you may hear those harpies' thrilling voices;
shout as you will, begging to be untied,
your crew must only twist more line around you
and keep their stroke up, till the singers fade.[1]

Despite Ulysses' violent struggles to pursue the voices once he heard them, his crew, following orders, tied him tighter, and rowed the ship safely out of danger. It was all in the planning.

But what would happen if it were left to Ulysses' Will?

This is the teaser set up by later poets. Samuel Daniel in the Elizabethan Age, and Tennyson in the Victorian, leave Ulysses free to choose, restrained this time only by the sinews of his own heroic heart. Not surprisingly, Ulysses triumphs over his passions—and gives the poets a chance to lay down a heavy moral theme.

Cream puts its money on the Sirens—along with about a thousand watts. A blinding sun shimmers across the cymbals, while the bass opens up a cataract and Clapton's seductive guitar weaves sinuous ribbons through our minds, luring us into an azure sea.

Somehow it is not dying, this. Or is it? The Sirens drive such speculation from our heads. This is *it*—the song, achingly close to the one Ulysses must have heard.

Yielding to the pull of Eros, we drown only to be reborn, escape only to find our Will is drowned, the last shred flowing into the unfathomable Cosmos.

This is not dying. Or is it?

Sustained in those passages which tell, at a lower pitch, of the

[1] From "The Sirens' Song," in Homer's *The Odyssey*, Book XII, translated by Robert Fitzgerald, copyright © 1961 by Robert Fitzgerald. Reprinted by permission of Doubleday & Company, Inc.

desire to return to the hard land of the winter, is a tension, not so much of moral struggle as the struggle of Hedonism to resist the total annihilation of Self in pleasure.

Homer was no stranger to that struggle. His descriptions of love and feasts, polished bronze and hot baths, abound in sensuality. Yet the appeal of his Sirens lies not in their sensuality, but in their skill with flattery. They begin by telling Ulysses that all the world knows of his glory and promise to regale him with stories of his exploits at Troy.

There is no escape from their dreaming. Their voices give shape to our innermost fantasies. Their green mirror irresistibly attracts the pathetic, isolated creature within us all.

No doubt about it: we can understand Homer better for having heard Cream. And the reverse. We might even ponder the question: If Homer's sound had gone through amplifiers first, would *The Odyssey* have been the richer or the poorer?

Tales of Brave Ulysses

ERIC CLAPTON and MARTIN SHARP

You thought the leaden winter
Would bring you down forever,
But you rode upon a steamer
To the violence of the sun.

And the colors of the sea
Find your eyes with trembling mermaids,
And you touch the distant beaches
With tales of brave Ulysses.

I was naked, ears were tortured
By the sirens sweetly singing,
For the sparkling waves are calling you
To kiss their white laced heads.

And you see a girl's brown body
Dancing through the turquoise,
And her footprints make you follow
Where the sky loves the sea.

And when your fingers find her
She drowns you in her body,
Carving deep blue ripples
In the tissues of your mind.

Tiny purple fishes
Run laughing through your fingers,
And you want to take her with you
To the hard land of the winter.

Her name is Aphrodite
And she rides a crimson shell,
And you know you cannot leave her
For you touch the distant sands.

With tales of brave Ulysses,
I was naked, ears were tortured
By the sirens sweetly singing.

Tiny purple fishes
Run laughing through your fingers,
And you want to take her with you
To the hard land of the winter.

The Sirens' Song

HOMER

This way, oh turn your bows,
  Akhaia's glory,
As all the world allows—
  Moor and be merry.

Sweet coupled airs we sing.
  No lonely seafarer
Holds clear of entering
  Our green mirror.

Pleased by each purling note
  Like honey twining
From her throat and my throat,
  Who lies a-pining?

Sea rovers here take joy
  Voyaging onward,
As from our songs of Troy
Greybeard and rower-boy
  Goeth more learned.

All feats on that great field
  In the long warfare,
Dark days the bright gods willed,
  Wounds you bore there,

Argos' old soldiery
  On Troy beach teeming,
Charmed out of time we see.
No life on earth can be
  Hid from our dreaming.

"Story of Issac," by Leonard Cohen, recorded on *Songs from a Room,* 1969

"The Parable of the Old Men and the Young," by Wilfred Owen (1893–1918), from *The Collected Poems of Wilfred Owen*

The story of Abraham and Isaac has fascinated listeners since even before the days of Homer. If the figure of the old man called upon by God to sacrifice his only son appears incomprehensible today, it is owing no more to Abraham's willingness to carry out the command than to the power of his love. We are more uncomfortable with it than ever. Yet the story endures, perhaps because human sacrifice endures; perhaps because that figure with the knife poised, appearing on so many stone lintels and in so many paintings, still stands after three thousand years as an index to our view of man.

The original story in the Old Testament is only eighteen lines of print.

Kierkegaard devoted a treatise toward unraveling its existential dilemma, and came to regard Abraham's faith with mixed awe. Eric Hoffer dismisses Abraham as a fanatic, the prototype of the True Believer. And in "Highway 61" Bob Dylan suggests that Abraham has no choice but to do the deed. In general the Twentieth Century has shifted its sympathies to Isaac. The poem by Wilfred Owen and the song by Leonard Cohen are no exceptions.

Wilfred Owen's poem, while adding details to make the identity of his Isaac clear, sticks fairly close to the original narrative. Until the stark twist of the ending.[2]

The original Abraham's hand was stopped, a ram offered in place of his son, and a Divine promise given to the old man that his descendants would prosper and multiply until they would be as numerous as the stars in the sky. Owen's Abraham declines to sacrifice his own Pride, and blindly destroys "half the seed of Europe."

Owen's rage against the First World War was founded on his own experience as a soldier. While a military stalemate lasted

[2] The sense of this last passage is conveyed especially well in Joan Baez's reading of the Owen poem on her album *Baptism: A Journey Through Our Time.*

from October 1914 to March 1918, with no attack moving the front more than 10 miles in either direction, leaders on both sides claimed to have "God on their side," and with patriotic fervor tried to capture a few yards of ground that might strengthen their prestige at the conference table in Paris. By the end of the war, the industrial power of several European nations had been destroyed, whole classes of people had been reduced to poverty, and ten million people had died.

The poet was killed in action on November 4, 1918, a week before the armistice was signed.

In 1968, Leonard Cohen used the story of Abraham and Isaac to convey the same theme. His handling of details is looser, but his final effect is the same, even to the assigning of blame to Pride, shown in the peacock spreading its fan.

What is distinctive about Cohen's "Story of Issac" are the shifts in point of view. He has divided the story into four equal parts. The narrative begins through the eyes of the boy "Issac," whose innocence and fidelity are reflected in his choice of images. In this first section the father is seen as self-righteous. It is not until the trek up the mountainside that the details of wine and vulture and the father's single backward glance open up the possibility of corruption.

Exactly halfway through, the narrative is interrupted by a mature "Issac," his life already spared, now as prophet testifying against those of the present age who appear to have confused military strategy with Divine Will. In the last section the speaker's identity is ambiguous, but there is no mistaking what will happen when it all comes down to dust. The voice in the last section is as pure in its cynicism as the first was in its innocence.

Story of Isaac

LEONARD COHEN

The door it opened slowly
My father he came in
I was nine years old

And he stood so tall above me
His blue eyes they were shining
And his voice was very cold

He said I've had a vision
And you know I'm strong and holy
I must do what I've been told

So we started up the mountain
I was running, he was walking
And his ax was made of gold

Well the trees they got much smaller
And the lake, a lady's mirror
We stopped to drink some wine

Then he threw the bottle over
It broke a minute later
Then he put his hand on mine

I thought I saw an eagle
But it might've been a vulture
I never could decide

Then my father built an altar
He looked once behind his shoulder
He knew I would not hide

You who build these altars now
To sacrifice these children
You must not build them any more

A scheme is not a vision
And you never have been tempted
By a demon or a God

You who stand above them now
Your hatchets blunt and bloody
You were not there before

When I lay upon the mountain
And my father's hand was trembling
With the beauty of the Word

And if you call me Brother
forgive me if I enquire
According to whose plan?

When it all comes down to dust
I will kill you if I must
I will help you if I can

When it all comes down to dust
I will help you if I must
I will kill you if I can

Have mercy on our uniform
Man of peace or man of war
The peacock spreads his fan

The Parable of the Old Men and the Young

WILFRED OWEN

So Abram rose, and clave the wood, and went,
And took the fire with him, and a knife.
And as they sojourned both of them together,
Isaac the first-born spake and said, "My Father,
Behold the preparations, fire and iron,
But where the lamb for this burnt-offering?"
Then Abram bound the youth with belts and straps,
And builded parapets and trenches there,
And stretched forth the knife to slay his son.
When lo! an angel called him out of heaven,
Saying, "Lay not thy hand upon the lad,
Neither do anything to him. Behold,
A ram, caught in a thicket by its horns;
Offer the Ram of Pride instead of him."
But the old man would not so, but slew his son,—
And half the seed of Europe, one by one.

"From the Underworld," by Howard Blaikley, recorded by
   The Herd as a single in 1967, and in the following year as an
   LP, entitled *Lookin Thru You*
"Orpheus and Eurydice," by Ovid (43 B.C.–A.D. 18), from
   Metamorphoses, translated by Rolfe Humphries

The taboo against "Looking Back" is as central to rock mythology as to the ancient. It was a matter of survival for the stars, once rock started changing rapidly during the mid-sixties. Bob Dylan ushered in a new kind of lyric. New familiarity with engineering techniques—multitracking, feedback control, etc.—opened up spectacular musical possibilities to the pop world. Virtuoso musicians were emerging as well, with guitarists such as Eric Clapton and Jimi Hendrix raising the calibre of playing so rapidly that a guitarist who was good in 1964 was going to have to work hard to stay good in 1968.

In the middle of it all came that phenomenally creative span of not quite two years, between the Beatles' release of *Rubber Soul* and *Magical Mystery Tour*, when every new album had to offer proof of continued growth. Past accomplishments were a trap. To look back was fatal.

Some of that tension flowed directly into the lyrics. And it was natural that songwriters should turn to legend to express a taboo. Cream's "Tales of Brave Ulysses" in a sense is about not looking back, about the allure of Sirens of one kind or another and the hard demands of schedules and craftsmanship. But the clearest counterpart in legend is Orpheus.

Orpheus, remember, was the young musician whose wife Eurydice died from a snakebite. Everyone is so paralyzed on Orpheus's playing that he gets permission to lead Eurydice from the Underworld, but he has to promise not to look back at her. To turn back the gaze is to lose the gift.

The story reaches us through the Latin poet Ovid, whose treatment of the Greek myth is simple. The psychology is transparent: Eurydice, dying a second time, has no complaint. Her husband, after all, had looked back in love. Yet those limpid verses contain room for complexity: Orpheus, by fearing she might falter, in a sense had lost faith: his love was corrupt, his nature too effeminate, to possess a love that was true.

Why did Orpheus look back? This is the heavy question for a later and Freudian age, so it is not surprising to find a rock treatment concerned with ulterior motives. An English teeny-bopper group called The Herd came out with a single called "From the Underground" that made the charts in 1967. We are treated to the picture of an Orpheus who looks back out of a perverse impulse and afterward analyzes his apparent need for self-destruction. The theme is so pat, the personalities so flimsy, that we cannot help wondering if the songwriter understood either Ovid or Freud. Or for that matter the milieu of the sixties.

Anyway, the parallel is there, and if nothing else it illustrates what happens when Neoclassicism gets hung up in the drapery folds and misses the spirit of its Classical subject.

From the Underworld

HOWARD BLAIKLEY

Out of the land of shadows and darkness
We were returning towards the morning light
Almost in reach of places I knew
Escaping the ghosts of yesterday

You were behind me following closely
Don't turn around now I heard you whisper in my ear
If you should turn now all that you've won
Will vanish just like a passing dream

Just on the very verge of the morning
Daylight was dawning, freedom was but a step away
Now with the deep dark river behind us
What could go wrong if I stayed strong in mind

What was the sudden lapse into madness
What was the urge that turned my head round to look at you
What was the stubborn will to destroy
the love and the joy I nearly held

Three times the thunder roar'd in my ears
in all of my years I'll see that lost look in your eyes
As with a sigh like smoke in the wind
you slipped from my grasp into the waiting shadows

So much I longed to say but my touch
found only the empty air and a black night's coldness
Into another world you have passed
and never again can I reclaim you

Orpheus and Eurydice

OVID

They climbed the upward path, through absolute silence,
Up the steep murk, clouded in pitchy darkness,
They were near the margin, near the upper land,
When he, afraid that she might falter, eager to see her,
Looked back in love, and she was gone, in a moment.
Was it he, or she, reaching out arms and trying
To hold or to be held, and clasping nothing
But empty air? Dying the second time,
She had no reproach to bring against her husband,
What was there to complain of? One thing, only:
He loved her. He could hardly hear her calling
Farewell! when she was gone.

      The double death
Stunned Orpheus, like the man who turned to stone
At sight of Cerberus, or the couple of rock,
Olenos and Lethaea, hearts so joined
One shared the other's guilt, and Ida's mountain,
Where rivers run, still holds them, both together.
In vain the prayers of Orpheus and his longing
To cross the river once more; the boatman Charon
Drove him away. For seven days he sat there
Beside the bank, in filthy garments, and tasting
No food whatever. Trouble, grief, and tears
Were all his sustenance. At last, complaining
The gods of Hell were cruel, he wandered on
To Rhodope and Haemus, swept by the north winds,
Where, for three years, he lived without a woman
Either because marriage had meant misfortune
Or he had made a promise. But many women
Wanted this poet for their own, and many
Grieved over their rejection. His love was given
To young boys only, and he told the Thracians

That was the better way: *enjoy that springtime,*
Take those first flowers!

Ancient sources figure in rock in a more general way, too.

Certain performers rely on ancient cultural symbols or per-
sonas—Donovan's attraction to gypsies and Jim Morrison's use of
the snake are two examples—and when these symbols are used
repeatedly by an artist and in a special relationship to each other,
then the artist is approaching the kind of personal mythology
evolved by such poets as Blake and Yeats.

The Beatles were doing this during their most creative period.
Interestingly, the submarine and people with blue faces, and a
land of free love, are all to be found in a medieval manuscript
called *King Alesaunder*. The theme of a land beneath the sea is
an ancient one, used by the Beatles to create a world of their own.

Other artists are more eclectic, drawing on existing religious
systems or pseudo-religious systems, such as Scientology, to create
such a world. Leonard Cohen is one. The Incredible String Band
is another, achieving at least one notable success in *The Hang-
man's Beautiful Daughter,* a difficult metaphysical patchwork
ordered around the Classical alchemy of Earth, Water, Fire and
Air.

With more simplicity, and razor intensity, Laura Nyro projects
a dark, jewel-like city of the soul, in which sensuality and evil
alternately struggle and combine. The streets are black; the devil
is sweet. In "Gibson Street" this landscape serves as the matrix for
an archetypal conflict, between a girl who once tasted of a for-
bidden berry and her desire to escape—first from an Underworld
by crossing a river, and then from the man who offered her the
fruit.

I sucked its juices never knowing
that I would sleep that night on Gibson Street

An early Homeric hymn tells the same story. Persephone was
raped by Hades, and because she had tasted a pomegranate seed,
was forced to remain with him in the Underworld for half the
year.

David Crosby's courtly "Guinnevere" recalls the lady of Arthurian legend. As in the Laura Nyro song, this appears to be a conscious allusion, integrated without pretense and with beautiful effect.

Paul Simon's "Sounds of Silence" shares with Psalm 115 [3] a protest against the idols of materialism whose silence turns their worshipers also silent. But where the psalm is a poetic argument for the existence of an intangible God, out of hands' reach, the song introduces a turned-up-collar Messiah who offers not only his wisdom but also his body. His rage belongs to a Moses upon discovering the waywardness of his followers, but his sensation trip is pure Jesus. In contrast to The Who's rock opera *Tommy*, its pinball Messiah preaching "See me, feel me, touch me," the sensuality creeps into the Simon and Garfunkel song softly, perhaps by accident. But "Sounds of Silence" is an honest song, and in its own way a classic.

When Simon turns to the psalms again with "Bridge over Troubled Water," mixing the theme of Psalm 23 with a broken metaphor and a swell of expansive church music, the effect is closer to Walt Disney.

Other songs have adapted ancient sources directly. To wit: *Joseph and His Many-Colored Dreamcoat* and *Jesus Christ Superstar* and Country Joe MacDonald's arrangements for the opera *Metamorphoses*. From The Rolling Stones' *Beggars' Banquet* album is a little-noticed (because almost unintelligibly sung) song called "Prodigal Son," written by the Reverend Robert Wilkins and paraphrasing the story from the Gospel according to Luke (15:11–32).

From the anonymous Middle English verse "Sumer is Icumen in" (ca. 1226), The Fugs fashioned a song called "Seize the Day," recorded on their first album. On their *Tenderness Junction* album, as part of "Aphrodite Mass," is a section entitled "Sappho's Hymn to Aphrodite," which is more fun than Classical.

From Ecclesiastes (3:1–8) Pete Seeger arranged a song popularized by The Byrds, called "Turn, Turn, Turn."

Finally, Dave van Ronk is emphatically a folk singer and wouldn't count here except that his treatment of Old Testament figures happens to achieve that uncanny *synch* with the present

[3] *The New English Bible* translation of Psalm 115 is preferable for clarity, while sacrificing none of the beauty of the King James.

that we lumber with clichés such as "timeless," etc., but can best define by listening. After the first few times around with "Mister Noah," you might find yourself thinking of those ads for bomb-shelters from the fifties, but almost anything from today's paper will do. That is the way Van Ronk's music works on you. Quietly. Humorously. His treatment of Samson straining at the temple pillars, though humorous, could not contrast more completely with Dylan's facetious handling of the same central figure in "Tombstone Blues." At the center of "Samson and Delilah," Van Ronk is in deadly earnest:

> If I had my way in this wicked world
> I'd tear this building down

And inextricably modern. Milton said it more grandly, but no more convincingly.

Loneliness
and
Love

EVERY love song conceals a song of loneliness; every song of loneliness, a song of love.

Baudelaire's "To the Reader" flows from such a vast loneliness it suggests a vast imagination for love—not necessarily a vast capacity; but at bottom it shares something in common with a work of such fierce love as Tim Hardin's *Suite for Susan Moore and Damion—We Are—One, One, All in One;* or with The Beatles' "In My Life," which is included in this next group of songs and poems.

Among the others, none can really be said to be totally about love or passion or loneliness. Each reflects the contradictions of life, the tensions which seem to plague everyone except those Beautiful Other People on television, the fugitives, the gutsy trial lawyers, the ecstatic consumers of soft drinks, deodorants and plastic hair sprays.

"Suzanne" is a great love song, even if the love portrayed is not a great love; because it takes its song life from the ambience of real life; because it catches a soul in the moment of hovering. Because it shows the ambivalence of "reaching out" for love.

"Four and Twenty," by Stephen Stills, recorded by
Crosby, Stills, Nash and Young on *Déja Vu*, 1970
"To the Reader," by Charles Baudelaire (1821–1867),
from *Les Fleurs du Mal*, 1857

Baudelaire's view of man contains an abyss. Start reading "To the
Reader" carefully, working your way down through the levels of
degradation, and feel your stomach lurch. And just when you
think there is an end to the "foul menagerie" of demons within our
brains, you are shown one more damned than all. The Churchman
would say Pride. Baudelaire says, *Boredom!* which

> Gladly of this whole earth would make a shambles
> And swallow up existence with a yawn. . . .

The abyss in Stephen Stills' song is not so wide, nor so clearly de-
fined. It is glimpsed but darkly, as someone gazing down at rotten
planks might discover the glitter of water far below. The hollow
center running through the father's life was disguised by material
striving; for the son it is disguised by a different longing. But the
way the two stories are told in tandem and the phrasing of the
son's questions leave little doubt that it is the same emptiness
within. Even the title recalls those blackbirds bursting forth from
their pie to sing anew.

Is Stills' abyss the same as Baudelaire's?

Stills chooses not to name his, leaving space for our minds to
roam. Nameless, it comes perhaps closer to another Baudelaire
poem, this one simply called "The Abyss." It picks up where the
other one left off and pursues things to their logical conclusion: If
all the little impulses of lust and repentance which jerk us like pup-
pets issue out of boredom, then beyond boredom is the ultimate
abyss—meaninglessness. Existence has already been swallowed
up with a yawn at the start of this poem. These are no demons
of our mere minds or denizens of some Dantean AAA-approved
Inferno—all safety of disguises has been swept away, all exits
sealed. It is the stark beginning of "All Along the Watchtower,"
except that Baudelaire keeps his promise, and instead of being
abandoned to phony innuendoes we are carried straightaway into

a demonic cosmos whose every cubic foot is the tracing of a "knowing" God, carried forward with the sheer force of an idea weaving like black lightning across the page and all the time knowing that somehow Baudelaire is doing this without any amplifier, with just language, kicking out the jambs and with the power of a few mindcrashing lines sweeping us onward and outward toward Edge City with our eyes wide open and no chorus to hang onto and no beat to lull us into a you-know-just-*feeling*-it stupor, and all the time the wide-open horror of that last line coming closer and closer. . . .

But it's a trip you have to take for yourself. Read "The Abyss." Listen to Stephen Stills singing "Four and Twenty" and hear "To the Reader." Then reread "The Abyss":

> Pascal's abyss went with him, yawned in the air,
> —Alas! All is abyss! Desire, act, dream,
> Word! I have felt the wind of Terror stream
> Many a time across my upright hair.
>
> Above, below, around me, shores descending . . .
> Silence . . . frightful, captivating Space . . .
> At night I watch God's knowing finger trace
> The dark with nightmare, multiform, unending.
>
> Sleep itself is an enormous lair,
> Filled with vague horror, leading none knows where;
> All windows open upon Infinity;
>
> My spirit, always haunted now by slumber,
> Yearns for extinction, insensibility.
> —Ah! never to be free of Being, Number! [4]

[4] "The Abyss," from Charles Baudelaire's *Flowers of Evil*, translated by Jackson Matthews. Copyright 1955 by New Directions Publishing Corporation. Reprinted by permission of New Directions Publishing Corporation.

Four and Twenty

STEPHEN STILLS

Four and twenty years ago a-comin to this life
The son of a woman and a man who lived in strife
    He was tired of being poor
    And he wasn't into sellin door to door
    And he worked like the devil to be more

A different kind of poverty now upsets my soul
Night after sleepless night I walk the floor and I want to know
    Why am I so alone?
    Where is my woman?
    Can I bring her home?
    Have I driven her away?
    Is she gone?

Morning comes the sunrise and I'm driven to my bed
I see that it is empty and there's devils in my head
    I embrace the many-colored beast
    I grow weary of the torment
    Can there be no peace?
    And I find myself just wishin
    That my life would soon decease

To the Reader

CHARLES BAUDELAIRE

Folly and error, avarice and vice,
Employ our souls and waste our bodies' force.
As mangy beggars incubate their lice,
We nourish our innocuous remorse.

Our sins are stubborn, craven our repentance.
For our weak vows we ask excessive prices.
Trusting our tears will wash away the sentence,
We sneak off where the muddy road entices.

Cradled in evil, that Thrice-Great Magician,
The Devil, rocks our souls, that can't resist;
And the rich metal of our own volition
Is vaporized by that sage alchemist.

The Devil pulls the strings by which we're worked:
By all revolting objects lured, we slink
Hellwards; each day down one more step we're jerked
Feeling no horror, through the shades that stink.

Just as a lustful pauper bites and kisses
The scarred and shrivelled breast of an old whore,
We steal, along the roadside, furtive blisses,
Squeezing them like stale oranges for more.

Packed tight, like hives of maggots, thickly seething,
Within our brains a host of demons surges.
Deep down into our lungs at every breathing,
Death flows, an unseen river, moaning dirges.

If rape or arson, poison, or the knife
Has wove no pleasing patterns in the stuff
Of this drab canvas we accept as life—
It is because we are not bold enough!

Amongst the jackals, leopards, mongrels, apes,
Snakes, scorpions, vultures, that with hellish din,
Squeal, roar, writhe, gambol, crawl, with monstrous shapes,
In each man's foul menagerie of sin—

There's one more damned than all. He never gambols,
Nor crawls, nor roars, but, from the rest withdrawn,
Gladly of this whole earth would make a shambles
And swallow up existence with a yawn . . .

Boredom! He smokes his hookah, while he dreams
Of gibbets, weeping tears he cannot smother.
You know this dainty monster, too, it seems—
Hypocrite reader!—You!—My twin!—My brother!

**"Suzanne," by Leonard Cohen, recorded on *Songs of
Leonard Cohen*, 1968
"Dover Beach," by Matthew Arnold (1822–1888), 1867**

Rivers have a way of forming channels in the mind. You can move
away from the river of your childhood but the magic remains. In
every poet's mind there is a river, running toward the sea.

Rivers, harbors, beaches. The tide. They ask more questions
than they answer. They are the great teachers.

Poets are forever returning to them.

In "Dover Beach," the stately rhythms of the full tide commu-
nicate the grandeur and sadness of England at the height of its
power; its ebbing foretells of a time of confusion, of "ignorant
armies" clashing by night.[5]

"Suzanne," with its mellifluous images of garbage and flowers,
portrays a world of decay and renewal.

Faith has retreated as a tide in Matthew Arnold's poem, just as
it appears "broken" in Cohen's second stanza, with Christ playing
the role of a lifeguard who is himself drowning.

What is left but love? And then to sort beauty from the chaos,
to find the heroes in the seaweed, to let the river answer.

Suzanne as Fool, defying the conventions of an uptight society,
recalls another heroine of poetry—W. B. Yeats' "Crazy Jane,"
whose lowly habits confound the Bishop no less than her hoary
ecology of love:

> ". . . Love has pitched his mansion in
> The place of excrement;
> For nothing can be sole or whole
> That has not been rent."

[5] The Fugs' handling of the last stanza on *Tenderness Junction* does special credit
to Arnold.

Cohen's lady understands the backside of the technocracy and the way to knowledge of Self, all in one; she holds up the mirror, for a generation of children to lean out for love. A new Madonna, more than any figure in rock she prefigures a generation literally engaged in recycling the waste of their parents' culture, in sorting through the rags and feathers and outworn creeds for something of beauty or use.

Suzanne

LEONARD COHEN

Suzanne takes you down
To her place near the river.
You can hear the boats go by,
You can stay the night beside her,
And you know that she's half-crazy
But that's why you want to be there,
And she feeds you tea and oranges
That come all the way from China,
And just when you mean to tell her
That you have no love to give her,
Then she gets you on her wave-length
And she lets the river answer
That you've always been her lover.

And you want to travel with her,
And you want to travel blind,
And you know that she can trust you
'Cause you've touched her perfect body
With your mind.

And Jesus was a sailor
When he walked upon the water
And he spent a long time watching
From a lonely wooden tower

And when he knew for certain
That only drowning men could see him,
He said, "All men shall be sailors, then,
Until the sea shall free them,"
But he, himself, was broken
Long before the sky would open.
Forsaken, almost human,
He sank beneath your wisdom
Like a stone.

And you want to travel with him,
And you want to travel blind,
And you think you'll maybe trust him
'Cause he touched your perfect body
With his mind.

Suzanne takes your hand
And she leads you to the river.
She is wearing rags and feathers
From Salvation Army counters,
And the sun pours down like honey
On our lady of the harbor;
And she shows you where to look
Among the garbage and the flowers.
There are heroes in the seaweed,
There are children in the morning,
They are leaning out for love,
And they will lean that way forever
While Suzanne, she holds the mirror.

And you want to travel with her,
You want to travel blind,
And you're sure that she can find you
'Cause she's touched her perfect body
With her mind.

Dover Beach

MATTHEW ARNOLD

The sea is calm tonight,
The tide is full, the moon lies fair
Upon the straits;—on the French coast the light
Gleams and is gone; the cliffs of England stand,
Glimmering and vast, out in the tranquil bay.
Come to the window, sweet is the night-air!
Only, from the long line of spray
Where the sea meets the moon-blanched land,
Listen! you hear the grating roar
Of pebbles which the waves draw back, and fling,
At their return, up the high strand,
Begin, and cease, and then again begin,
With tremulous cadence slow, and bring
The eternal note of sadness in.

Sophocles long ago
Heard it on the Aegean, and it brought
Into his mind the turbid ebb and flow
Of human misery; we
Find also in the sound a thought,
Hearing it by this distant northern sea.

The Sea of Faith
Was once, too, at the full, and round earth's shore
Lay like the folds of a bright girdle furled.
But now I only hear
Its melancholy, long, withdrawing roar,
Retreating, to the breath
Of the night-wind, down the vast edges drear
And naked shingles of the world.

Ah, love, let us be true
To one another! for the world, which seems
To lie before us like a land of dreams,
So various, so beautiful, so new,

Hath really neither joy, nor love, nor light,
Nor certitude, nor peace, nor help for pain;
And we are here as on a darkling plain
Swept with confused alarms of struggle and flight,
Where ignorant armies clash by night.

"Albatross," by Judy Collins, recorded on *Wildflowers*, 1967
"Patterns," [6] by Amy Lowell (1874–1925), from *Men,*
    Women and Ghosts, 1916

Both ladies are imprisoned, the one in her stiff brocade, the other behind the isinglass windows of her eyes, within a charmed circle of filigree.

The enchantment might be broken by the arrival of the soldier, heavy-booted, the sun flashing from his sword-hilt; or by the prince on his splashing steed, holding the sun in his hands. The imagery is strikingly parallel.

Both visions are summoned up from water—that most sensuous medium, but with its dual capacity either to nurture or to destroy, expressed mythically in the idea of Aphrodite being born from seafoam, and in the myth of Narcissus falling in love with his own image reflected in water and drowning.

Enter the heroes, both dazzling, Apollonian, crashing forward in exuberance with arms outstretched—yet both are hopelessly romanticized and one of them is dead; so in fantasy they will reach out forever, arms never closing, forever dissolving against the mundane pattern of garden paths and servants and effete young men bearing violets. The circle remains unbroken: the garden paths will find with snow and still the footsteps will go on pacing; and at night the iron wheels will roll relentlessly toward the sea.

Listen to Judy Collins sing "Albatross." Listen to "Patterns" read aloud by a beautiful woman.

---

[6] Paul Simon has written his own "Patterns," recorded on *Parsley, Sage, Rosemary and Thyme.*

Albatross

JUDY COLLINS

The lady comes to the gate,
Dressed in lavender and leather
Looking North to the sea
She finds the weather fine,
She hears the steeple bells—
Ringing through the orchard
All the way from town.
She watches seagulls fly
Silver on the ocean
Stitching through the waves
The edges of the sky.
Many people wander up the hills from all around you,
Making up your memories and thinking they have found you.
They cover you with veils of wonder
As if you were a bride,
Young men holding violets are curious
To know if you have cried,
And tell you why and ask you why, any way you answer.
Lace around the collars of the blouses of the ladies,
Flowers from a Spanish friend of the family,
The embroidery of your life
Holds you in and keeps you out but you survive,
Imprisoned in your bones
Behind the isinglass windows of your eyes,

And in the night the iron wheels
   rolling through the rain,
Down the hills through the long grass
   to the sea,
And in the dark the hard bells
   ringing with pain,
Come away alone . . .
Come away alone . . . with me.

Even now by the gate
With your long hair blowing,
And the colors of the day
That lie along your arms,
You must barter your life
To make sure you are living,
And the crowd that has come,
You give them the colors,
And the bells and wind and the dreams.
Will there never be a prince
Who rides along the sea and the mountains,
Scattering the sand and foam
Into amethyst fountains,
Riding up the hills from the beach
In the long summer grass,
Holding the sun in his hands
And shattering the isinglass?
Day and night and day again,
And people come and go away forever,
While the shining summer sea
Dances in the glass of your mirror,
While you search the waves for love
And your visions for a sign,
The knot of tears around your throat
Is crystalizing into your design . . .

And in the night the iron wheels
    rolling through the rain
Down the hills through the long grass
    to the sea,
And in the dark the hard bells
    ringing with pain,
Come away alone . . .
Come away alone . . . with me.

Patterns

AMY LOWELL

I walk down the garden paths,
And all the daffodils
Are blowing, and the bright blue squills.
I walk down the patterned garden paths
In my stiff, brocaded gown.
With my powdered hair and jeweled fan,
I too am a rare
Pattern. As I wander down
The garden paths.

My dress is richly figured,
And the train
Makes a pink and silver stain
On the gravel, and the thrift
Of the borders.
Just a plate of current fashion,
Tripping by in high-heeled, ribboned shoes.
Not a softness anywhere about me,
Only whalebone and brocade.
And I sink on a seat in the shade
Of a lime tree. For my passion
Wars against the stiff brocade.
The daffodils and squills
Flutter in the breeze
As they please.
And I weep;
For the lime tree is in blossom
And one small flower has dropped upon my bosom.

And the plashing of waterdrops
In the marble fountain
Comes down the garden paths.
The dripping never stops.

"Patterns," by Amy Lowell, from *The Complete Poetical Works of Amy Lowell*.
Reprinted by permission of Houghton Mifflin Company.

Underneath my stiffened gown
Is the softness of a woman bathing in a marble basin,
A basin the midst of hedges grown
So thick, she cannot see her lover hiding,
But she guesses he is near,
And the sliding of the water
Seems the stroking of a dear
Hand upon her.
What is Summer in a fine brocaded gown!
I should like to see it lying in a heap upon the ground.
All the pink and silver crumpled up on the ground.

I would be the pink and silver as I ran along the paths,
And he would stumble after,
Bewildered by my laughter.
I should see the sun flashing from his sword-hilt and
   the buckles on his shoes.
I would choose
To lead him in a maze along the patterned paths,
A bright and laughing maze for my heavy-booted lover
Till he caught me in the shade,
And the buttons of his waistcoat bruised my body as
   he clasped me,
Aching, melting, unafraid.
With the shadows of the leaves and the sundrops,
And the plopping of the waterdrops,
All about us in the open afternoon—
I am very like to swoon
With the weight of this brocade,
For the sun sifts through the shade.

Underneath the fallen blossom
In my bosom
Is a letter I have hid.
It was brought to me this morning by a rider from the Duke.
"Madam, we regret to inform you that Lord Hartwell
Died in action Thursday se'nnight."
As I read it in the white, morning sunlight,
The letters squirmed like snakes.

"Any answer, Madam," said my footman.
"No," I told him.
"See that the messenger takes some refreshment.
No, no answer."
And I walked into the garden,
Up and down the patterned paths,
In my stiff, correct brocade.
The blue and yellow flowers stood up proudly in the sun,
Each one.
I stood upright too,
Held rigid to the pattern
By the stiffness of my gown;
Up and down I walked,
Up and down.

In a month he would have been my husband.
In a month, here, underneath this lime,
We would have broke the pattern;
He for me, and I for him,
He as Colonel, I as Lady,
On this shady seat.
He had a whim
That sunlight carried blessing.
And I answered, "It shall be as you have said."
Now he is dead.

In Summer and in Winter I shall walk
Up and down
The patterned garden paths
In my stiff, brocaded gown.
The squills and daffodils
Will give place to pillared roses, and to asters, and to snow.
I shall go
Up and down
In my gown.
Gorgeously arrayed,
Boned and stayed.
And the softness of my body will be guarded from embrace
By each button, hook, and lace.

For the man who should loose me is dead,
Fighting with the Duke in Flanders,
In a pattern called a war.
Christ! What are patterns for?

**"In My Life," by John Lennon and Paul McCartney,
  recorded on *Rubber Soul*, 1965
"The Old Familiar Faces," by Charles Lamb (1775–1834),
  from *The Oxford Book of English Verse*, 1900**

Here are two works, one from the eighteenth century and the other by The Beatles, which deal with love and friendship in relation to memories of the past.

Each may be accused of being sentimental to the point of maudlin. Yet the past is felt as an immense weight in each. Once you get past the annoyance of Lamb's refrains, and irritation with a mind that lives so deeply in the past, then you see that his anguish is real, and that his present friend can *never* share his memories; and the haunted refrain begins to run like the scenario of a Fellini movie. By contrast it is we who live in the present whose lives may appear bare.

The Beatles song, which Judy Collins took for the title of an album, reveals the same tension. In its promise for the future, it is a love song. But the promise conceals pain and the knowledge that the future draws its credit from the past.

Nostalgia was unhip during the Rock Revolution of the sixties, which makes this song all the rarer; a chance to pause with The Beatles, on the brink of that next rushing step from *Rubber Soul* to *Revolver*, and to look back on the people and places left behind.

In My Life

JOHN LENNON and PAUL McCARTNEY

There are places I'll remember all my life,
Though some have changed, some forever, not for better,
Some have gone and some remain.
All these places had their moments
With lovers and friends I still can recall.
Some are dead and some are living. In my life I've loved them
    all.
But of all these friends and lovers,
There is no one compares with you,
And these mem'ries lose their meaning
When I think of love as something new.
Though I know I'll never lose affection
For people and things that went before,
I know I'll often stop and think about them,
In my life I'll love you more.
Though I know I'll never lose affection
For people and things that went before,
I know I'll often stop and think about them,
In my life I'll love you more. In my life I'll love you more.

The Old Familiar Faces

CHARLES LAMB

I have had playmates, I have had companions,
In my days of childhood, in my joyful school-days—
All, all are gone, the old familiar faces.

I have been laughing, I have been carousing,
Drinking late, sitting late, with my bosom cronies—
All, all are gone, the old familiar faces.

"In My Life," by John Lennon and Paul McCartney. Reprinted from *The Beatles Illustrated Lyrics* by permission of Delacorte Press/A Seymour Lawrence Book.

I loved a Love once, fairest among women:
Closed are her doors on me, I must not see her—
All, all are gone, the old familiar faces.

I have a friend, a kinder friend has no man:
Like an ingrate, I left my friend abruptly;
Left him, to muse on the old familiar faces.

Ghost-like I paced round the haunts of my childhood,
Earth seem'd a desert I was bound to traverse,
Seeking to find the old familiar faces.

Friend of my bosom, thou more than a brother,
Why wert not thou born in my father's dwelling?
So might we talk of the old familiar faces—

How some they have died, and some they have left me,
And some are taken from me; all are departed—
All, all are gone, the old familiar faces.

SORROW associated with death is a frequent theme in poetry as in the blues. Yet it largely disappears in rock—a fact owing not to any apparent optimism in the pop scene, nor to any obvious delicacy of taste. Murder receives its plays, as in "Sympathy for the Devil" and "Maxwell's Silver Hammer"; and in the earlier protest songs the circumstances of a particular death are used to make a point. At the other extreme, saccharine deaths are used to push records like "Honey" to the top of the singles charts.

What is missing is a contemplative view of death.

Among the several tempting explanations, one is the youth of the artists. But Bryant philosophized about death in "Thanatopsis" when he was seventeen; and Keats' death elicited more response from his fellow poets, most of them in their twenties and thirties, than all the combined deaths of pop stars have elicited so far.

Do we value human life more cheaply today?

Is youth worried less about death, or worried more?

Or is rock simply one more adjunct of a depersonalized society, which—fed on a diet of violence—can pick up a gun and inflict death more easily than it can mourn it?

During the protest era of the early sixties sorrow was politicized, crowded out by a smoldering rage. Two songs, both sung by Pete Seeger, are direct heirs of Lord Byron's angry "Who Killed John Keats?"—one written by Norman Rosten about the death of Marilyn Monroe, called "Who Killed Norma Jean"; the other, an early Dylan song about prize fighting called "Who Killed Davy Moore?" Neither is without poignancy; and in "The Lonesome Death of Hattie Carroll," Dylan constructs a brittle melodrama from the facts. But pathos is not sorrow, as the hip title of the last one suggests. And none are really rock.

Simon and Garfunkel come closer to hard rock with their "Richard Cory," but if you compare it with Dave van Ronk's "He Was a Friend of Mine," you see how really political it is. "He Was a Friend of Mine" responds to a death personally and with disarming simplicity. But Van Ronk's song is folk.

In "I Shall Not Care," Tom Rapp takes a Sara Teasdale poem, splits it in half, and inserts some lines from Roman tombs along with scraps of *Peer Gynt* set to hard rock. The resultant collage appears in *Pearls Before Swine*—a courageous effort—but the song behaves less like rock than a treatise on heart stoppage.

More convincing is Paul Simon's "So Long, Frank Lloyd Wright." Half tongue-in-cheek, yet wistful, the song reminisces over the late architect's genius.

> I'll remember Frank Lloyd Wright
> All of the nights we'd harmonize till dawn.

A perfect counterpart to the elegy of traditional poetry, the song takes refuge in hip irony, but it somehow escapes sounding embarrassed, and its softly contemplative mood offers proof that the taboo can be broken. Yet its reduced tempo is a reminder that once again we are dealing with a song somewhere out on the periphery.

The closer we get to the center of the mainstream, the less room rock seems to have for sorrow.

It is as though a generation, emotionally self-indulgent in other ways, had cut itself off from sorrow. Anger, yes. Compassion, sometimes. But sorrow never—and excluded with it, a rich stratum of related emotions.

Or else it is something to do with rock itself.

The power of hard rock to express emotions of anger, joy, passion, anxiety—or at least certain *kinds* of anger, joy, passion and anxiety—is formidable by any artistic standard. Just as obviously we can see that to subject "He Was a Friend of Mine" to a throbbing bass would destroy the quiet candor of Van Ronk's song. To inject a raunchy phrasing or hyped-up backing into "The Lonesome Death of Hattie Carroll" would be grotesque. Hard rock tends to impose extremity on mood.

Whatever the reasons, if the kind of sorrow we have been talking about is an unsuitable subject for rock, then perhaps rock has served as a *refuge from death.* And—at least during the sixties—a refuge from the claims of sentiment.

The formal question remains: *Is hard rock capable of dealing with death except in violent terms?*

The response of the human animal to death within his own species is basic, surely. Throughout literature we find room for quiet affections, powerful spiritual love, solitary doubts; resonance for the nuances of emotions recollected in tranquility—and by no means unrelated to this, a large number of poems responding quietly to death; even the death of someone known only distantly by the poet. The response is not always one of sorrow. Frost's "Death of a Hired Man" reveals a complex and often ironic attitude that has little to do with grief or sentiment and everything to do with compassion and some unnamable center of the soul. To read it is to become more human.

Ultimately the question concerns the breadth and sensitivity of rock as a medium of artistic expression—the range it offers a generation.

No attempt is made here to provide answers. But here are two songs relevant to the asking. Each attempts something rare—to deal in its own way with death, within the emotional confines prescribed by rock.

"Casey Jones," by Robert Hunter, recorded by The Grateful Dead on *Workingman's Dead*, 1970 "Joseph Mica," an anonymous Negro ballad associated with the "Casey Jones" of Walsh Saunders, ca. 1900

The ballad of Casey Jones was inspired by an actual wreck on the Illinois Central line. On a murky night, April 29, 1900, the "Cannonball" pulled out of Memphis with a string of passenger cars, ninety-five minutes behind schedule. Seeing as how engine 382 was steaming unusually well, engineer Casey Jones tried to make up the lost time along a 100-mile straightaway. A lantern flashed, warning of a freight disabled ahead. Whether Casey ever saw the signal is unclear, but when the fireman yelled the freight was only a few hundred feet away. Casey told him to jump, and stayed to cut his speed in the seconds remaining before he plowed into the other train. The only one killed was Casey. He was found in the wreck with one hand still clutching the whistle cord, the other holding the air brake hose.

Casey had been as colorful a figure as he was punctual. He stood six feet four, his special six-tone calliope whistle was famous all down the line, and naturally the story of his heroism traveled. But it remained for a black man to turn Casey into a legend. Walsh Saunders, an engine wiper, put the exploits of the hero into a chanty, which got sung around stoves and in bars frequented by railroad men until it reached the ears of some white songwriters, who polished it and turned it into a hit. It is this Tin Pan Alley version that has the familiar chorus:

> Casey Jones, mounted to the cabin,
> Casey Jones, with his orders in his hand,
> Casey Jones, mounted to the cabin,
> And he took his farewell trip to the promised land.

Walsh Saunders' original song is lost. But folklorists believe it was based on an older song called "Jimmie Jones," which a friend of Saunders had heard years before in Kansas City from a strolling street guitarist. Only fragments of "Jimmie Jones" survive, but the name appears in the second stanza of another Negro ballad,

"Joseph Mica," which may take us closer to Saunders' original "Casey Jones."

The Grateful Dead's song shares with those earlier fragments of "Casey Jones" the same outward simplicity; the short, driving lines, the imperfect rhymes, and the understated mood.

But underneath the down-home facade, the Dead are devious. Each line is broken in half and set rolling—lurching forward and backward, against the insistent tempo of the bass; while the lugubrious backbeat, growing steadily more compulsive, the increasingly livid images impaled on a spiraling internal rhyme scheme, the mind-ratcheting repetition, all serve to underscore the fact that our hero is wrecked on cocaine. Looming outside of time, the engine "just gleams," a phantom spliced into Casey's fantasy.

The rock song, like its folk counterpart, is based on fact—the death of Neal Cassady, reputedly the real-life model for "Dean Moriarty," the rollicking Zen freak who madly talks and steals cars while blitzing his way like a comet through the pages of Jack Kerouac's *On the Road.* His presence is felt in the racing pulse of Allen Ginsberg's *Howl.* By the time he appears under his own name in Tom Wolfe's *The Electric Kool-Aid Acid Test,* Cassady's mind has overrevved and is devoted to the repetition of flipping a sledgehammer into the air and catching it, but the quest is the same.

> . . . he is both a head whose thing is speed,
> meaning amphetamines, and a unique being whose
> quest is Speed, faster goddamn it, spiraling,
> jerking, kicking, fibrillating tight up against
> the 1/30 of a second movie-screen barrier of our
> senses, trying to get into . . . *Now—*[7]

Either way, speed killed. In February, 1967, Neal Cassady was found in Mexico alongside a railroad track, dead apparently of heart failure.

Both ballads, then, use real events to portray a hero so hung up on Time as to finally merge his identity with the machine. All

[7] Tom Wolfe, *The Electric Kool-Aid Acid Test* (New York: Farrar, Straus & Giroux), 1968.

Joseph Mica wants is "water'n coal." All Casey wants is to make it on time.

And at this point the song by Robert Hunter may be said to part company with the older ballad, because his true subject is Time—his object being the destruction of linear Time. And this places his "Casey Jones" in the tradition of the elegy, a poem which uses the occasion of someone's death to express first grief and then faith in the immortality which will transcend death. Two classic examples of English elegies are Thomas Gray's "Elegy Written in a Country Churchyard," and Shelley's long poem, "Adonais," written on the occasion of Keats' death.

The Dead's "Casey" unfolds (without ever unfolding—and this is precisely the point) a slow-motion explosion of the moment of truth. We brace ourselves for the crash that never comes, because that engine "just gleams" and the chorus enfolds us in the time preceding the crash; approaching it again, we see that the bend is a parabolic curve, and the closer we approach the moment of impact the more everything slows down, until it is all frozen in the strobelight repetition of the chorus—fragments of life and death interfaced in a mosaic outside of time, in a wreck that never was because it is; and we are forever crashing, trapped somewhere within that 1/30-second time lag between the fact and the knowledge of death. Our own death will never have any more reality for us than right now, in our imaginations. The last line of the chorus reminds us that the whole reality of the song—life and death alike—is a notion that just crossed the singer's mind, and is just now crossing the listener's mind.

Casey Jones

ROBERT HUNTER

Driving that train, high on cocaine
Casey Jones you'd better watch yo' speed
Trouble ahead, trouble behind
And you know that notion just crossed my mind

"Casey Jones," lyrics by Robert Hunter, © Ice Nine Publishing Co., 1971. Reprinted by permission.

This old engine makes it on time
Leave at the station about a quarter to nine
Hit Trouble Junction at seventeen to
At a quarter to ten you know it's driving again

(*Chorus*)

Trouble ahead—uh, Lady in Red
Take my advice you'd be better off dead
Switchman sleeping, train hundred and two
is on the wrong track and headin' for you

(*Chorus*)

Trouble with you is the trouble with me
Got two good eyes but they still don't see
Come round the bend you know it's the end
But the fireman screams and the engine just gleams

(*Chorus*)
(*Chorus*)

Joseph Mica

ANONYMOUS

Joseph Mica was good engineer,
Tole his fireman not to fear.
All he want is water'n coal,
Poke his head out, see drivers roll.

Early one mornin' look like rain,
'Round de curve come passenger train.
On powers lie ole Jim Jones,
Good ole engineer, but daid an' gone.

"Joseph Mica," anonymous, from "Folk-song and Folk-poetry as Found in Secular Songs of the Southern Negroes," by Howard W. Odum, in *Journal of American Folklore*, volume 24, page 352, 1911, Reprinted by permission of The American Folklore Society, Inc.

Left Atlanta hour behin',
Tole his fireman to make up the time.
All he want is boiler hot,
Run in there 'bout four o'clock.

"Bishop Cody's Last Request," by Tom Paxton, recorded
    on *The Things I Notice Now*, 1969
"The Bishop Orders His Tomb at Saint Praxed's Church,"
    by Robert Browning (1812–1889), from *Dramatic*
    ***Romances and Lyrics*, 1845**

"The Bishop Orders His Tomb at Saint Praxed's Church" is one
of the more complex poems in this collection, but at its core is the
situation portrayed in Tom Paxton's song: a dying bishop attempts
to work his will on the living. Gathered around the bishop are his
nephews and illicit sons, by his brother's wife. The poem is a
dramatic monologue, and we hear only the bishop's discourse,
which mainly concerns his tomb, how he wants it to be con-
structed of the finest marble and set with a piece of *lapis lazuli*,
a costly blue stone, so as to eclipse the tomb of his old rival, Gandolf, who lives buried opposite in a sepulcher made of an inferior
marble, called onion-stone because it peels in layers.

As the bishop rambles, other threads entwine—the story of Old
Gandolf cozening him out of the burial niche in the south corner
of the church; and the secret of the lump of *lapis lazuli*, which the
bishop had buried following a fire, and which is to be his final
triumph—the crowning thread in the web of jealousy and intrigue
which has sustained the bishop all his life.

Fear that his request may not be carried out rises to despera-
tion toward the end of his monologue. But he finds solace in his
one immutable triumph: the memory of how Gandolf always
envied him his mistress.

Death as the ultimate defining act, the power of dying hours to
summon the true priorities, is a tradition which has served Shakespeare to dramatic advantage and saved the sheepherders from
the cattlemen more than once. A dying man always tells the truth.

Just as our answer to the question "What would we do if we knew we had only a week to live?" tells a truth about our lives.

In the final workings of Browning's bishop's mind we see old friends and old enemies become distinguishable. Hate can be as sustaining as love.

In Tom Paxton's song, the dying bishop's obsession suggests he is the prisoner of some doubt. He suddenly wants to see the brother to whom he had only sent birthday cards. Perhaps he loved his brother all along. Or perhaps, as the opening stanza suggests, he wants to bring his brother before him in order to judge him. But why this dying need to impose a judgment?

As in the poem, the darkest features of the portrait emerge from what is absent from that last request.

"Thanks for all the birthday cards" is a cheerful reminder of the gulf of space and time with which the two brothers separated themselves all along. The older brother might as easily have been an executive at IBM; the birthday cards would be no less patronizing. The younger brother refuses to patronize him in return.

In the final stanza of Paxton's song the bishop's death becomes a camp *cause célèbre*—his reward, the opening of a new bar in the Haight—like the sweating sandstone tomb envisioned by his counterpart.

Ironically it is the younger brother who grants a kind of absolution.

> His brother told the priest, "The Bishop rests in peace.
> He never failed me."

Bishop Cody's Last Request

TOM PAXTON

Bishop Cody's last request
Was wired across the sea:
"Find my wandering brother, Boys,
And bring him home to me.

I knew him as an infant,
As a meek and trusting child;
But lately I've had sad reports
My brother is running wild.
Oh, bring my brother home to me,
With my own eyes I've got to see
Just what he's into."

Bishop Cody's last request
Received respectful care.
The trail said, "California,"
And they found his brother there.
They found him in an alley,
In a sea of broken glass.
They plucked him from the traffic
Of the hustlers tripping past.
"Oh, Sir, your brother's eyes are dim,
We've come to take you home to him.
He needs to see you."

Bishop Cody's last request
Was told in great detail.
The messengers were desperate men,
They had not come to fail.
They pressed their case with fervor,
Their urgency was clear,
While Bishop Cody's brother smiled
And did not seem to hear.
"Oh, give the Bishop my regards,
Thanks for all the birthday cards,
He never failed me."

Bishop Cody's messengers
Were left with no recourse.
The situation plainly called
For a little use of force.
They grabbed him by the shoulder,
But the shoulder slipped away.
As he vanished down the alley

They could hear the brother say,
"Oh, give the Bishop my regards,
Thanks for all the birthday cards,
He never failed me."

Bishop Cody's last request
Was broadcast through the town,
And Bishop Cody's brother
Was quite often seen around.
The messengers were frantic,
Quite efficient and discreet,
But their manner grew distracted
When they saw him on the street.
"Oh, Sir, you have to go,
Oh, Sir, at least you owe
An explanation."

Bishop Cody's last request
Was finally denied.
As his spirit left his body
Someone heard: "My hands were tied."
The word went down the alley
That the Bishop was at rest,
And someone opened up a bar
Called The Bishop's Last Request.
His brother told the priest,
"The Bishop rests in peace.
He never failed me."

The Bishop Orders His Tomb
at Saint Praxed's Church

ROBERT BROWNING

Vanity, saith the preacher, vanity!
Draw round me bed: is Anselm keeping back?
Nephews—sons mine . . . ah, God, I know not! Well—

She, men would have to be your mother once,
Old Gandolf envied me, so fair she was!
What's done is done, and she is dead beside,
Dead long ago, and I am Bishop since,
And as she died so must we die ourselves,
And thence ye may perceive the world's a dream.
Life, how and what is it? As here I lie
In this state chamber, dying by degrees,
Hours and long hours in the dead night, I ask
"Do I live, am I dead?" Peace, peace seems all.
Saint Praxed's ever was the church for peace;
And so, about this tomb of mine, I fought
With tooth and nail to save my niche, ye know:
—Old Gandolf cozened me, despite my care;
Shrewd was that snatch from out the corner south
He graced his carrion with, God curse the same!
Yet still my niche is not so cramped but thence
One sees the pulpit o' the epistle side,
And somewhat of the choir, those silent seats,
And up into the aery dome where live
The angels, and a sunbeam's sure to lurk:
And I shall fill my slab of basalt there,
And 'neath my tabernacle take my rest,
With those nine columns round me, two and two,
The odd one at my feet where Anselm stands:
Peach-blossom marble all, the rare, the ripe
As fresh-poured red wine of a mighty pulse.
—Old Gandolf with his paltry onion-stone,
Put me where I may look at him! True peach,
Rosy and flawless: how I earned the prize!
Draw close: that conflagration of my church
—What then? So much was saved if aught were missed!
My sons, ye would not be my death? Go dig
The white-grape vineyard where the oil-press stood,
Drop water gently till the surface sink,
And if ye find . . . Ah God, I know not, I! . . .
Bedded in store of rotten fig leaves soft,
And corded up in a tight olive-frail,
Some lump, ah God, of *lapis lazuli,*

Big as a Jew's head cut off at the nape,
Blue as a vein o'er the Madonna's breast . . .
Sons, all have I bequeathed you, villas, all,
That brave Frascati villa with the bath,
So, let the blue lump poise between my knees,
Like God the Father's globe on both his hands
Ye worship in the Jesu Church so gay,
For Gandolf shall not choose but see and burst!
Swift as a weaver's shuttle fleet our years:
Man goeth to the grave, and where is he?
Did I say basalt for my slab, sons? Black—
'Twas ever antique-black I meant! How else
Shall ye contrast my frieze to come beneath?
The bas-relief in bronze ye promised me,
Those Pans and Nymphs ye wot of, and perchance
Some tripod, thyrsus, with a vase or so,
The Saviour at his sermon on the mount,
Saint Praxed in a glory, and one Pan
Ready to twitch the Nymph's last garment off,
And Moses with the tables . . . but I know
Ye mark me not! What do they whisper thee,
Child of my bowels, Anselm? Ah, ye hope
To revel down my villas while I gasp
Bricked o'er with beggar's moldy travertine
Which Gandolf from his tomb-top chuckles at!
Nay, boys, ye love me—all of jasper, then!
'Tis jasper ye stand pledged to, lest I grieve
My bath must needs be left behind, alas!
One block, pure green as a pistachio nut,
There's plenty jasper somewhere in the world—
And have I not Saint Praxed's ear to pray
Horses for ye, and brown Greek manuscripts,
And mistresses with great smooth marbly limbs?
—That's if ye carve my epitaph aright,
Choice Latin, picked phrase, Tully's every word,
No gaudy ware like Gandolf's second line—
Tully, my masters? Ulpian serves his need!
And then how I shall lie through centuries,
And hear the blessed mutter of the mass,

And see God made and eaten all day long,
And feel the steady candle flame, and taste
Good strong thick stupefying incense-smoke!
For as I lie here, hours of the dead night,
Dying in state and by such slow degrees,
I fold my arms as if they clasped a crook,
And stretch my feet forth straight as stone can point,
And let the bedclothes, for a mortcloth, drop
Into great laps and folds of sculptor's-work:
And as yon tapers dwindle, and strange thoughts
Grow, with a certain humming in my ears,
About the life before I lived this life,
And this life too, popes, cardinals, and priests,
Saint Praxed at his sermon on the mount,
Your tall pale mother with her talking eyes,
And new-found agate urns as fresh as day,
And marble's language, Latin pure, discreet
—Aha, ELUCESCEBAT quoth our friend?
No Tully, said I, Ulpian at the best!
Evil and brief hath been my pilgrimage.
All *lapis*, all, sons! Else I give the Pope
My villas! Will ye ever eat my heart?
Ever your eyes were as a lizard's quick,
They glitter like your mother's for my soul,
Or ye would heighten my impoverished frieze,
Piece out its starved design, and fill my vase
With grapes, and add a vizor and a Term,
And to the tripod ye would tie a lynx
That in his struggle throws the thyrsus down,
To comfort me on my entablature
Whereon I am to lie till I must ask
"Do I live, am I dead?" There, leave me, there!
For ye have stabbed me with ingratitude
To death—ye wish it—God, ye wish it! Stone—
Gritstone, a-crumble! Clammy squares which sweat
As if the corpse they keep were oozing through—
And no more *lapis* to delight the world!
Well go! I bless ye. Fewer tapers there,
But in a row: and, going, turn your backs

—Aye, like departing altar-ministrants,
And leave me in my church, the church for peace,
That I may watch at leisure if he leers—
Old Gandolf, at me, from his onion-stone,
As still he envied me, so fair she was!

Tigers
of
Wrath

PROTEST and alienation are so much a part of our milieu that we have no adequate words to describe them. Like the Eskimos who have no single word for snow, we have no words for the anger that has increasingly permeated the past 175 years.

For the past century the history of movements within poetry has been largely the search for fresh modes of protest as the old forms are exhausted. As Romanticism becomes outworn, we turn to realism, then to surrealism, then to Dada, and then to a revival of some previous form.

In the midsixties the form and the mode and the word seemed to be Rock. But it was also a commercial medium, and the fact that it stood not only for protest and alienation but also for big money seemed to doom it to quick decay. The "works of alienation"—fulfilling Herbert Marcuse's prediction—were absorbed by society for its entertainment. "Thus they become commercials—they sell, comfort, or excite." [8] This packaging process may have been aided by the additional factor of catharsis, which explains more convincingly than any politics of ecstasy why all that freaky laughter, that madcap exuberance of psychedelia should have burst forth for a period coinciding exactly with the greatest escalation of American troops in Viet Nam.

[8] Herbert Marcuse, *One Dimensional Man* (Boston: Beacon Press), 1964.

By late 1968, it seemed as though one more mode of protest had been exhausted. Psychedelia would be looked back on as a nightmare.

At the same time, the rapid spread of this exhaustion to almost all quarters of rock, and the fact of it all coinciding with the sense of futility that descended over the protest movement at large, emphasizes one thing characteristic of the new music: whatever its drawbacks as a form, whatever its ambivalence between protest and catharsis, rock was founded on intense social concern. Not only was Dylan's "It's All Over Now, Baby Blue" as much protest as his earlier "Masters of War," but also it is this background social concern, as much as anything, that distinguishes American rock from English. It explains why that period of greatest ferment, for all its strung-out, presumably apolitical inward trippiness, defies comparison with the hallucinatory visions of Rimbaud, Coleridge and Poe; why the Americans, with their satirical edge, are much closer to the political visionaries, Blake, Shelley and Lewis Carroll.

Another observation comes to light when we examine rock from the perspective of traditional poetry: while many of the protests are not new, none of the poems included in this section go back further than two centuries. Blake, Shelley, Baudelaire, Whitman, Yeats, cummings, Allen Ginsberg, Gary Snyder, Bob Dylan, Frank Zappa, were and are the vanguard poets of essentially the same revolution.

"Masters of War," by Bob Dylan, recorded on *Freewheelin'*
   Bob Dylan, 1963
"England in 1819," by Percy Bysshe Shelley (1792–1822),
   written in 1819

Raging against the old men who make the wars, Shelley and Dylan are Furies who pursue the objects of their hatred to the grave.

Shelley's personal attack on George III, beginning

   "An old, mad, blind, despised and dying king . . ."

is unmatched by anything in rock, for sheer vitriolic intensity. The fumbling king, his lineage, and then the very *idea* of a king, are attacked in a series of devastating images. While the camera zooms yet further away, the scene of desolation broadens, becoming in the final couplet a graveyard from which a Phantom may burst forth to illuminate a New Age.

The rhetoric is congenial to rock; the same progression is found in Paul Kantner's "Crown of Creation," and the images of decay in Frank Zappa's work. Shelley's scorn is matched, if not with the same formal intensity, by the cheerful irony of Country Joe's "I-Feel-Like-I'm-Fixin'-To-Die Rag." But the closest single parallel is Dylan's "Masters of War."

Dylan faced a diffuse target. After all, The War had been mechanized and bureaucratized from the bright uniforms and chess maneuvers of Shelley's day into the Kafkan horror marketed on today's television, winding up in our cereal bowls.

Whom was the songwriter to attack?

The corporate Milo Minderbinders who sell napalm for bombing and then sell surgical jelly for treating the burns? The Draft Board? Those university professors who quietly contracted to write Cambodian language-instruction manuals six months before the invasion of Cambodia?

Dylan brushes these complexities aside, and goes after the perennial Old Man—my old man, your old man, Jim Morrison's old man—only *this time he's wearing a mask and he's pulling the strings and*—and that's about as far as the allegory goes. Because where Shelley's field of vision widens to encompass some of the complexities of his world, Dylan's rambling stanzas never quite get past that first painfully simple accusation; the cartoon grave where the old villain is dying probably of apoplexy. And you knew it was too easy. The real villain is out there still, on Desolation Row. But remember this was 1963 and nobody was laying down any very heavy raps in music, at least as far as white kids could tell.

As for the Utopian hope expressed in Shelley's final image, we had to wait four years for songs like Tim Buckley's "Goodbye and Hello," but the glimpse was there: the phantom of our opera, folk singer *cum* Avatar of the New Age, Dylan pointing at the grave of the old culture.

Masters of War

BOB DYLAN

Come you masters of war
You that build all the guns
You that build the death planes
You that build the big bombs
You that hide behind walls
You that hide behind desks
I just want you to know
I can see through your masks

You that never done nothin'
But build to destroy
You play with my world
Like it's your little toy
You put a gun in my hand
And you hide from my eyes
And you turn and run farther
When the fast bullets fly

Like Judas of old
You lie and deceive
A world war can be won
You want me to believe
But I see through your eyes
And I see through your brain
Like I see through the water
That runs down my drain

You fasten the triggers
For the others to fire
Then you set back and watch
When the death count gets higher
You hide in your mansion
As young people's blood

Flows out of their bodies
And is buried in the mud

You've thrown the worst fear
That can ever be hurled
Fear to bring children
Into the world
For threatenin' my baby
Unborn and unnamed
You ain't worth the blood
That runs in your veins

How much do I know
To talk out of turn
You might say that I'm young
You might say I'm unlearned
But there's one thing I know
Though I'm younger than you
Even Jesus would never
Forgive what you do

Let me ask you one question
Is your money that good
Will it buy you forgiveness
Do you think that it could
I think you will find
When your death takes its toll
All the money you made
Will never buy back your soul

And I hope that you die
And your death'll come soon
I will follow your casket
On a pale afternoon
And I'll watch while you're lowered
Down to your death bed
And I'll stand o'er your grave
Till I'm sure that you're dead.

England in 1819

PERCY BYSSHE SHELLEY

An old, mad, blind, despised, and dying king—
Princes, the dregs of their dull race, who flow
Through public scorn—mud from a muddy spring;
Rulers who neither see, nor feel, nor know,
But leechlike to their fainting country cling,
Till they drop, blind in blood, without a blow;
A people starved and stabbed in the untilled field—
An army, which liberticide and prey
Makes as a two-edged sword to all who wield;
Golden and sanguine laws which tempt and slay;
Religion Christless, Godless—a book sealed;
A Senate—Time's worst statute unrepealed—
Are graves, from which a glorious Phantom may
Burst, to illumine our tempestuous day.

"The Fool on the Hill," by John Lennon and Paul
   McCartney, from The Beatles' *Magical Mystery Tour*, 1967
"The Dawn," by William Butler Yeats (1865–1939),
   from *The Wild Swans at Coole*, 1919

One refuge against pedantry has always been to proclaim ignorance. To honor the Fool is to protest the authority of reason.

The "ignorance" of Yeats' poem is the ignorance of the stars, navigating the vast millennia, heedless of the petty empires of man. His contempt is for the man whose response to beauty is to run out and start measuring its parts. The same distrust for scientific observation was voiced a century earlier by Blake, who saw the perception of the senses as leading to something greater—the unseen Whole, arrived at not by deduction but by a flash of intuition. Blake had visions. Yeats had poetry. Squinting, he could imagine the dawn riding in the sun chariot, Helios "rocking the glittering coach above the cloudy shoulders of the horses." It was as real as mathematical formulae used to describe the same thing.

In a sense this is the story of the Romantic movement, this preference for personification in an increasingly depersonalized age.

The Fool, as a personification of this kind of "ignorance," is a standard figure in folklore. The Trickster-Hero was always playing the fool to con the wielders of power and escape with the bacon. The prophets of Apollo at the temple at Delphi were often recruited from among backward folk, and the Fool in Tarot prophecy is often the card played last. During the Middle Ages people thought that lunatics and fools had special soothsaying powers. These and a host of other folk practices, including the crowning of fools as Lords of Misrule, combined protest against authority and a belief, popularly held up until the time of the Industrial Revolution, that wisdom implied a measure of folly.

"The Fool on the Hill" raises an old emblem in protest against a Technocracy which, rational in all its parts, and proceeding scientifically according to impersonalized decision-making processes and cost-efficiency analysis, appears well on its way to stripping the planet of human life.

The Beatles' fool is unliked and presumably wise for one reason: he perceives the Whole. He sees the world spinning round. He is a man of a "thousand voices," plural both in the sense of representing a whole movement and by refusing to adhere to a single rationalized point of view.

This is the flip side of Calvinism, and it spins around with calculated ease. Perhaps too calculated. The lyrics are sparse, offering no argument or compelling images. The song, by taking its applause for granted, illustrates the artistic as well as the political dangers of the Fool's withdrawal.

The Fool on the Hill

JOHN LENNON and PAUL McCARTNEY

Day after day, alone on a hill,
the man with the foolish grin is keeping
perfectly still.
But nobody wants to know him,
they can see that he's just a fool
and he never gives an answer.
But the fool on the hill sees the sun going
down
and the eyes in his head see the world
spinning round.
Well on the way, head in a cloud,
the man of a thousand voices talking
perfectly loud.
But nobody ever hears him
or the sound he appears to make
and he never seems to notice.
But the fool on the hill sees the sun
going down
and the eyes in his head see the world
spinning round.
And nobody seems to like him,
they can tell what he wants to do
and he never shows his feelings.
But the fool on the hill sees the sun going
down
and the eyes in his head see the world
spinning round.
He never listens to them,
he knows that they're the fools.
They don't like him.
The fool on the hill sees the sun going
down

"The Fool on the Hill," by John Lennon and Paul McCartney. Reprinted from *The Beatles Illustrated Lyrics* by permission of Delacorte Press/A Seymour Lawrence Book.

and the eyes in his head see the world
spinning round.

The Dawn

WILLIAM BUTLER YEATS

I would be ignorant as the dawn
That has looked down
On that old queen measuring a town
With the pin of a brooch,
Or on the withered men that saw
From their pedantic Babylon
The careless planets in their courses,
The stars fade out where the moon comes,
And took their tablets and did sums;
I would be ignorant as the dawn
That merely stood, rocking the glittering coach
Above the cloudy shoulders of the horses;
I would be—for no knowledge is worth a straw—
Ignorant and wanton as the dawn.

"The Continuing Story of Bungalow Bill," by John Lennon
and Paul McCartney, recorded on *The Beatles*, 1968
"buffalo bill's," by e. e. cummings (1894–1962), from
Collected Poems 1923–1954, 1923

A century ago William Frederick Cody (1846–1917) rode to fame
on a watersmooth-silver stallion and the pseudonym of Buffalo
Bill. His thing was killing buffalo. He killed them at the rate of
about 250 a month, mostly by contract with the railroads and the
U.S. Army.

Then about fifty years ago the poet e. e. cummings got hold of what had become a legend ☆ ☆ ☆ ☆ Buffalo Bill's Wild West Show ☆ ☆ ☆ ☆ because Cody had capitalized on his reputation as buffalo hunter and Indian fighter, formed a circus and toured all over America and Europe for the past forty years, and the image of a big horse rearing back and a rider with both guns blazing was now a glamorous part of the national pantheon of heroes. Cummings, returning home disillusioned with the Great War, looked at that image and pronounced it defunct.

Not dead, but defunct.

Cummings' choice of that word suggests he was talking not about old William Cody, who had expired a few years before, but about an enterprise and a mentality that had outrun its usefulness.

The poem, with its rearing typography, its onetwothreefourfive pigeons cascading across the page, has become a modern classic. What is overlooked sometimes, in all that exuberance, is the meaning at the core of the legend.

Buffy Sainte-Marie's song, "Now That the Buffalo's Gone," wrenches the fact of the slaughter away from history and reminds us that treaties are being broken today, that genocide is a continuing fact.

But the glamour also continues, mainly the property of white American males over fifty. In every President's boyhood surely dwells a hopelessly secret sweaty dream from off the thumb-soiled covers of a zillion dime novels, of a magnificent white horse rearing back, and astride him with a gun blazing in each hand— ☆ ☆ ☆ ☆ Okay, so they couldn't become Buffalo Bill; they had to settle for second best. But the fantasy hangs yet in the closet collecting dust, waiting for the magic word.

Defunct, but not dead.

It is the fantasy shorn of its glamour that The Beatles reintroduce fifty years after cummings' poem, with "The Continuing Story of Bungalow Bill." Whether the word *continuing* is intended to suggest a sequel to cummings' poem or the continuance of the fantasy, prolonged involvement of troops in Viet Nam, the allegorical meaning is precise: Bungalow Bill's thing is still killing, only he has been graduated to an elephant and a cast of thousands, and with the approval of Mum England he pursues the Tiger into the jungle. There he is taken by surprise. Tonkin, the magic word, brings reinforcements in the person of Captain Marvel, the continuing aggressive fantasy of a younger generation.

Brattishly singsong, the lyrics fade into a chorus of whistles with a bungling horn threading its way through scattered applause; and, halfway into the next track, a resounding "Heil!"

The Continuing Story of Bungalow Bill

JOHN LENNON and PAUL McCARTNEY

Hey, Bungalow Bill
What did you kill
Bungalow Bill?
He went out tiger hunting with his elephant and gun
In case of accidents he always took his mom
He's the all-American bullet-headed saxon mother's son.
All the children sing
Hey, Bungalow Bill
What did you kill
Bungalow Bill?
Deep in the jungle where the mighty tiger lies
Bill and his elephants were taken by surprise
So Captain Marvel zapped in right between the eyes
All the children sing
Hey, Bungalow Bill
What did you kill
Bungalow Bill?
The children asked him if to kill was not a sin
Not when he looked so fierce, his mother butted in
If looks could kill it would have been us instead of him
All the children sing
Hey, Bungalow Bill
What did you kill
Bungalow Bill?

buffalo bill's

e. e. cummings

Buffalo Bill's
defunct
    who used to
    ride a watersmooth-silver
                   stallion
and break onetwothreefourfive pigeonsjustlikethat
                                   Jesus

he was a handsome man
                   and what i want to know is
how do you like your blueeyed boy
Mister Death

"Pictures of a City," by Robert Fripp and Peter Sinfield, recorded by King Crimson on *In the Wake of Poseidon*, 1970
"London," by William Blake (1757–1827), from *Songs of Experience*, 1794

Rock does not lack for romantic views of the city. Joni Mitchell's "Night in the City" and Laura Nyro's "New York Tendaberry" convey a sense of the city as an almost religious experience. Even John Sebastian's "Summer in the City," for all its images of grit and sound of pneumatic drill, catches the uptempo excitement of the city in heat.

But for Robert Fripp and Peter Sinfield of King Crimson, the city is a collision of flesh and concrete. Steel and glass, flashing lights and the squeal of brakes are strung together in a cacophonous computer printout. The words are chanted, boxed within the framework of a few blaring notes. Only the last instrumental interlude offers any peace, and then we are returned with more deadening effect to the lockstep madness. It is reminiscent of Fritz Lang's science fiction film classic, *Metropolis*.

Blake's "London" marks the same woe, but in human faces, voices, sighs and curses. The sounds are human sounds. And the manacles are forged by human minds, maintained by human institutions.

Both works lean heavily on the technique of synecdoche, the use of a fragment to suggest the whole, as for instance King Crimson uses the phrase

pasteboard time slot sweat and spin

to suggest a sensory picture of a factory assembly line. But while King Crimson uses the technique for aesthetic reasons, for Blake it expresses his philosophical imperative: the existence of a single individual victimized by society is a blight upon the whole society. The difference is a key one.

While King Crimson attacks the bad vibes of the city, the noise and the alienation, the city as an unpleasant place for nice people to live, Blake is attacking institutionalized poverty.

Chimney sweeps in the eighteenth century were apprenticed at a young age, deprived of education, and usually died of congestion in the lungs and skin diseases. They were victims of a system of apprenticeship which was supported in turn—like the institution of prostitution—by the class system and by the powerful collusion of Church and State; just as infants today attacked in their cribs by rats or starved of protein are victims not only of slumlords and price fixing in the ghetto, but of the pattern of discrimination in the larger society.

Blake is saying—incredibly, for his times—that the existence of one child chimney sweep, one child maimed by a rat, is an indictment against all of us.

Life goes on. It is estimated 14,000 children and adults are bitten by rats in the United States annually. Rock stars continue getting upwards of $30,000 for concert performances. And the only ones writing songs anymore about rats devouring children are relatively unknown black singers like Leon Thomas.

Pictures of a City

ROBERT FRIPP and PETER SINFIELD

Concrete cold face cased in steel
Stark sharp glass-eyed crack and peel
Bright light scream beam brake and squeal
Red white green white neon wheel.

Dream flesh love chase perfumed skin
Greased hand teeth hide tinseled sin
Spice ice dance chance sickly grin
Pasteboard time slot sweat and spin.

Blind stick blind drunk cannot see
Mouth dry tongue tied cannot speak
Concrete dream flesh broken shell
Lost soul lost trace lost in hell.

London

WILLIAM BLAKE

I wander thro' each charter'd street,
Near where the charter'd Thames does flow,
And mark in every face I meet
Marks of weakness, marks of woe.

In every cry of every Man,
In every Infant's cry of fear,
In every voice, in every ban,
The mind-forg'd manacles I hear.

How the Chimney-sweeper's cry
Every black'ning Church appalls;
And the hapless Soldier's sigh
Runs in blood down Palace walls.

But most thro' midnight streets I hear
How the youthful Harlot's curse
Blasts the new born Infant's tear,
And blights with plagues the Marriage Hearse.

"The Observation," by Donovan Leitch, recorded on
   Mellow Yellow, 1967
"Ye Hasten to the Grave!" by Percy Bysshe Shelley
   (1792–1822), 1820

Haste, a purposeless bustle toward death, are parts of the vision shared by Donovan in "The Observation," and Shelley in his sonnet.

The word "thing" is used blankly in both works, to suggest this vacuous intent, a generalized state of mind which is blind to the specifics of either sidewalk or "green and pleasant path."

Seeking in the wrong places, the harried people in Shelley's poem find refuge in the "cavern of gray death," just as Donovan's T.V. commentators "give out the news that the world's got the blues" and the audience takes refuge in the media.

Conformity prompts the haste in both poem and song. The idle brains whom Shelley addresses wear the "world's livery," and the moviegoers whom Donovan observes "get by on the great community lie," not having space in their lives to act on their own impulses.

The difference is that Shelley's people rush to inquire and possess. Donovan's people have everything, including easy answers.

The Observation

DONOVAN LEITCH

On the sidewalk the people are bustling,
they ain't got no time so they think on the thing
that will fill in the space in between birth and death;
Who're they kidding.

On the T V the people are mumbling and grumbling,
they ain't got no hope so they give out the news
that the world's got the blues,—S O S, S O S.—
Bless my soul.

In the movies the people are identifying,
they ain't got no season to split for no reason
and so they get by on the great community lie.—
Who're they kidding,
Who're they kidding.

Ye Hasten to the Grave!

PERCY BYSSHE SHELLEY

Ye hasten to the grave! What seek ye there,
Ye restless thoughts and busy purposes
Of the idle brain, which the world's livery wear?
O thou quick heart, which pantest to possess
All that pale Expectation feigneth fair!
Thou vainly curious mind which wouldest guess
Whence thou didst come, and whither thou must go,
And all that never yet was known would know—
Oh, whither hasten ye, that thus ye press,
With such swift feet life's green and pleasant path,
Seeking, alike from happiness and woe,
A refuge in the cavern of gray death?
O heart, and mind, and thoughts! what thing do you
Hope to inherit in the grave below?

Prophetic
Voices

VIOLENT revolution was starting to seem all but inevitable in the late sixties, and a growing note of destruction was sounded in rock. Surprisingly, among all those spokesmen for the Apocalypse, among the hairiest prognosticators of doom, the chief voice remains that of W. B. Yeats.

His brooding fascination for astrology, his turning toward the East for inspiration and renewal, his contempt for cash-register morality and fingers that "fumble in the greasy till," and his ambivalent responses toward the revolution in Ireland anticipate part of the temper of youth today. Most of all, his premonitions of disaster expressed in the system of occult symbols—Moon and Blood, Tower, Falcon—have been invoked as eagerly by *Time-Life* mythographers as by soothsayers on the New Left.

Joan Didion entitled a foreboding collection of essays *Slouching Toward Bethlehem*, after Yeats' poem.

Richard Fariña, in "The Falcon," uses the image of the bird in a manner reminiscent of Yeats. Another Fariña song, "Michael, Andrew and James," recalls Yeats' "September 1913."

Phil Ochs called his song about the tear gas and violence at the Democratic National Convention in Chicago in 1968 "William Butler Yeats Visits Lincoln Park and Escapes Unscathed," but his invocation of Yeats is more than sardonic; not only the images of tower and "blood-red moon" but also Ochs' own anguish on that album reflect Yeats—a partisan conscience torn by events. The refrain goes,

> Through Lincoln Park the dark was turning, turning,

suggesting, along with Ochs' "Another Age," the cyclical view of history held by Yeats.

The moon, according to Yeats, in its twenty-eight phases signals a rise and decline in man's fortunes, ascending from the new moon to heroism in the twelfth moon, to the frenzy of the full moon, and declining into the age of Hunchback and Saint and Fool—an age of sickness and death. Following the darkness at the bottom of the cycle is renewal. This cycle takes place within a larger counterpart cycle, in which the Christian millennium is to be followed 2,000 years later at the opposite turn of the wheel, by a Second Coming, a terrible birth bringing darkness and dissolution.

Considered in Yeatsean terms, Jim Morrison's demonology becomes clearer. When Morrison sings of "the end" he is referring not just to a trip, and the dissolution of ego, but to the destruction of an age, an approaching darkness which is at once terrible and welcome,

> . . . the end of laughter, and soft lies.

A Roman wilderness . . . all the children insane . . . a migration along the highways West, riding the blue bus toward the cataclysmic destruction. And perhaps rebirth, but that is not the Trip—the Trip is destruction.

An early Morrison poem, "Horse Latitudes," bears an uncanny—probably wholly unconscious—similarity to an early Yeats poem, "He Bids His Beloved Be at Peace."

The list could go on. The point is Yeats is the special patron of the Apocalyptic vision in rock today. And the three songs that follow are no exceptions.

**"Bad Moon Rising," by John Fogerty, recorded by Creedence Clearwater Revival as a single, 1969
"Dirge," by Percy Bysshe Shelley (1792–1822), from *Poems Written in 1822***

A bad moon rising—this one in John Fogerty's song—is used by Creedence Clearwater Revival to warn the listener directly, and thereby capitalize on the special goosebumps that inevitably accompany such auguries; recalling Caesar's ill-fated visit to the Senate, the prophecies that California will slip into the sea, and the omens in *Easy Rider;* and convincing us, in case we didn't already know, that man never outgrows his primitive credulity.

If it is not blood on the moon, it is the toothpaste that will bring romance, or the spaceflight that will restore national virility. We live by charms.

"Bad Moon Rising" may only pander to the audience's paranoia; certainly it offers nothing new in the way of insights. But then neither does Shelley's poem. Both are simple outcries, incantatory, using sound to evoke a simple but intense emotion.

Bad Moon Rising

JOHN FOGERTY

I see a bad moon rising,
I see trouble on the way,
I see burnt wakes of lightning,
I see bad times today

Don't go round tonight,
They're bound to take your life,
There's a bad moon on the rise.

85

I hear hurricanes a-blowing,
I know the end is coming soon,
I feel rivers overflowing,
I hear the voice of wreckage and ruin.

Well, don't go round tonight,
Well, it's bound to take your life,
There's a bad moon on the rise.

Hope you got your things together,
Hope you are quite prepared to die,
Looks like we're in for nasty weather,
"What now!", You're thinking for a night.

A Dirge

PERCY BYSSHE SHELLEY

Rough wind, that moanest loud
   Grief too sad for song;
Wild wind, when sullen cloud
   Knells all the night long;
Sad storm, whose tears are vain,
Bare woods, whose branches strain,
Deep caves and dreary main,—
   Wail, for the world's wrong!

"Stories of the Street," by Leonard Cohen, recorded
   on *Songs of Leonard Cohen*, 1968
"The Second Coming," by William Butler Yeats
   (1865–1939), from *Michael Robartes and the Dancer*, 1921

Chaos expanding with the falcon's widening circles, passions
reeling beyond reason's control, circles turning within the larger
cycle—Yeats' poem portrays a world spinning like a gyroscope

whose axis is tilting ever closer to the point of no return. The hope raised for a savior is met instead with the birth of a hybrid monster with gaze "blank and pitiless as the sun."

For Leonard Cohen, too, the center is eroding, of a society polarized as Ireland was. In Yeats, "The best lack all conviction, while the worst are full of passionate intensity." In Cohen, "The middle men are gone" and "The cities are broke in half."

Instead of growing, the schism is already wide at the beginning of Cohen's song. Cadillacs creep through poison gas in Spanish Harlem. The progression in Cohen's song is uncertain, the imagery sometimes fractured, threading through streets and highways and one-night hotels, to the pastoral salvation which turns out to be as bogus as the hoped-for Second Coming—an effort at pastoral lobotomy which offers no real alternative for urban man.

The larger cycle of Yeats' poem is broken up in Cohen's song, where each stanza oscillates on its separate axis, between death and the hope for renewal; between the suicide and the rose, the hexagram and the girl.

As for the lady with the classy legs and steering wheel, maybe that's Our Lady of the Harbor, with one more pair of wire wheels bearing down on her; but the image suggests a chrome-bosomed technocracy, McLuhan's Mechanical Bride careening in slow motion into the abyss. Cohen's imagery seems prone to skid in this song—"apples to keep animals warm"?—but the next curve compensates: the infant hauled in like a kite, "one eye filled with blueprints and one eye filled with night," fills in the sense of hybridization, and the Picasso-like fragmentation which is partly what the song is about; the intrusion of mechanism, the age of lust giving birth to a computer.

Stories of the Street

LEONARD COHEN

The stories of the street are mine
The Spanish voices laugh
The Cadillacs go creeping down
Through the night and the poison gas
I lean from my window sill
In this old hotel I chose.
Yes, one hand on my suicide
And one hand on the rose.

I know you've heard it's over now
And war must surely come,
The cities they are broke in half
And the middle men are gone.
But let me ask you one more time
O children of the dust,
These hunters who are shrieking now
Do they speak for us?

And where do all these highways go
Now that we are free?
Why are the armies marching still
That were coming home to me?
O lady with your legs so fine
O stranger at your wheel
You are locked into your suffering
And your pleasures are the seal.

The age of lust is giving birth
But both the parents ask the nurse
To tell them fairy tales on both sides of the glass
Now in the infant with his cord
Is hauled in like a kite
And one eye filled with blueprints
One eye filled with night.

O come with me my little one
And we will find that farm
And grow us grass and apples there
To keep all the animals warm
And if by chance I wake at night
And I ask you who I am
O take me to the slaughter house
I will wait there with the lamb.

With one hand on a hexagram
And one hand on a girl
I balance on a wishing well
That all men call the world
We are so small between the stars
So large against the sky
And lost among the subway crowds
I try to catch your eye.

The Second Coming

WILLIAM BUTLER YEATS

Turning and turning in the widening gyre
The falcon cannot hear the falconer;
Things fall apart; the centre cannot hold;
Mere anarchy is loosed upon the world,
The blood-dimmed tide is loosed, and everywhere
The ceremony of innocence is drowned;
The best lack all conviction, while the worst
Are full of passionate intensity.

Surely some revelation is at hand;
Surely the Second Coming is at hand.
The Second Coming! Hardly are those words out

When a vast image out of *Spiritus Mundi*
Troubles my sight: somewhere in sands of the desert
A shape with lion body and the head of a man,
A gaze blank and pitiless as the sun,
Is moving its slow thighs, while all about it
Reel shadows of the indignant desert birds.
The darkness drops again; but now I know
That twenty centuries of stony sleep
Were vexed to nightmare by a rocking cradle,
And what rough beast, its hour come round at last,
Slouches towards Bethlehem to be born?

"The King Must Die," by Bernie Taupin, recorded on
   ***Elton John,* 1970**
"The Death of Kings," by William Shakespeare
   (1564–1616), from *King Richard II,* ca. 1596

Graves . . . worms . . . rainy eyes. . . . Sodden images are
used in the opening lines of Edward's speech to set a cheerless
stage for talk about the death of kings. Some riffs about regicide
lead into the central figure of Death playing the jester within the
mortal temples of a king; and then the scene of pomp, developed
by Shakespeare in a leisurely way within images of concentric
circles, is ended with a little pin.

Recalling how the whole scene would have been enacted in
Elizabethan days within a wooden circle, we sense the further
irony of Shakespeare as omniscient jester, commanding all with
playwright's pen.

Words like *pen* and *temple* with double entendre, and funny
creations like "monarchize," are part of Shakespeare's special
resonance. Reading the poem, you can hear him snickering gently
outside the circle of your gaze.

The trouble with Bernie Taupin playing Shakespeare is that
some of those lines sound so portentous, rolling off the tongue
with the heft of pure gold, and leaving the listener with the im-

pression of containing half of the world's wisdom—and a suspicion that this is exactly what we are supposed to believe.

Nuggets like these—"Some men are better staying sailors" is another—are tossed along the way with a deliberation calculated to pique the listener into thinking it *must mean something* (like what kind of double entendre can you make of *alter*), but they don't bear scrutiny and the whole thing lacks the playfulness of the Beatles' lyrics, where you know they are playing and they know you know it. It has the cold glint of market research.

It would be easier to write off Bernie Taupin's lyrics as a travesty of Shakespeare and the Elton John production as a slick *John Wesley Harding* formula, if the performance didn't somehow muster such emotional impact. After a few listenings to "The King Must Die," you realize that most of the time the lyrics are serving in only the most abstract way to guide the emotional flow of Elton John's voice.

The first stanza, by establishing a compact dramatic situation, serves as a valve to funnel the rest of the song, with its veiled allusions to courtiers and mercenaries and ostlers. It is like pulling the bathtub stopper out of *Macbeth.*

Good clean fun. And when you have watched all the seas incarnadine go sliding past, and the last line with its invocation of the sacrificial cycle swirling everything around in a tortuous final loop, you are left with the bathtub, property of Mary Renault, installed by James Frazer, decor by W. B. Yeats.

The King Must Die

BERNIE TAUPIN

No man's a jester playing Shakespeare
Round your throne room floor
While the juggler's act is danced upon
The crown that you once wore.

And sooner or later,
Everybody's kingdom must end,
And I'm so afraid your courtiers,
Cannot be called best friends.

Caesar's had your troubles
Widows had to cry
While mercenaries in cloisters sing
And the King must die.

Some men are better staying sailors
Take my word and go
But tell the ostler that his name was
The very first they chose.

And if my hands are stained forever
And the altar should refuse me
Would you let me in, would you let me in,
Should I cry sanctuary.

Caesar's had your troubles
Widows had to cry
While mercenaries in cloisters sing
And the King must die.

No man's a jester playing Shakespeare
Round your throne room floor
While the juggler's act is danced upon
The crown that you once wore.

The King is dead
The King is dead
The King is dead
Long Live the King.

The Death of Kings

WILLIAM SHAKESPEARE

Let's talk of graves, of worms, and epitaphs.
Make dust our paper, and with rainy eyes
Write sorrow on the bosom of the earth . . .
For God's sake, let us sit upon the ground,
And tell sad stories of the death of kings:
How some have been deposed; some slain in war;
Some haunted by the ghosts they have deposed;
Some poisoned by their wives; some sleeping killed;
All murdered:—for within the hollow crown
That rounds the mortal temples of a king
Keeps Death his court; and there the antick sits,
Scoffing his state, and grinning at his pomp;
Allowing him a breath, a little scene,
To monarchize, be feared, and kill with looks;
Infusing him with self and vain conceit—
As if this flesh, which walls about our life,
Were brass impregnable; and humored thus,
Comes at the last, and with a little pin
Bores through his castle-wall, and—farewell king!

Anthems
of the
New
Republic

EVERY movement has its official anthem, just as it has its unofficial anthem. Joni Mitchell's "Woodstock" is probably the first kind of anthem. Dylan's "New Morning" is the other.

Walt Whitman, like Thoreau, sang under his own private banner. But that was okay, because his song included everybody. His was the first Alice's Restaurant Massacree Movement, and people are still joining.

Walk on the grass and you are walking on Walt Whitman. He loves it.

Get high on *Leaves of Grass.*

A new vision seems to be in the making. Rock is less concerned these days with bending minds than with the task of rebuilding heads. Thoughtful days, these; and like *New Morning,* the Grateful Dead's *Workingman's Dead* is an uncanny and beautiful album to come along when it did; the opening cut, "Uncle John's Band," reflects in images of the rising tide that whole mellowing process that has gone on in the afterglow of *Sergeant Peppers.* It is a thoughtful album, about wheels and time and a lot of good things—including the burdens of the Scene. At the end of "New Speedway Boogie," Robert Hunter's lyrics go,

> One way or the nother
> This darkness got to give.

Here are some songs from other albums—all of them recent—that entertain a new dawn; songs that include one battle hymn, and a couple of others that can only be termed religious.

"Father of Night," by Bob Dylan,
  from *New Morning*, 1970
Song of Myself (22), by Walt Whitman (1819–1892),
  first published in 1855

Someone has called Dylan's "Father of Night" a stern testament of Calvinism. The fact is, it shares more in common with some of the prayer-chants of the Hopis or with the ancient benedictions to Odin the All-Father of Nordic belief, or the Brahmanic hymns.

In the *Bhagavad Gita*, Krishna speaks:

> I am the Father of this universe, and even the Source of the Father. I am the Mother of his universe, and the Creator of all. I am the Highest to be known, the path of purification, the holy OM, the Three Vedas.

> I am the Way, and the Master who watches in silence; thy friend and thy shelter and thy abode of peace. I am the beginning and the middle and the end of all things: their seed of Eternity, their Treasure supreme.

> The heat of the sun comes from me, and I send and withhold the rain. I am life immortal and death; I am what is and I am what is not.[9]

The idea of a god of a million faces—father of contradictions; of evil as well as good—is embraced by William Blake's *Songs of Innocence* and *Songs of Experience*. And in "Proverbs of Hell,"

[9] *The Bhagavad Gita* (9:17–19), translated by Juan Mascaró, copyright © Juan Mascaró 1962. Used by permission of Penguin Books Ltd.

Blake says things like "The lust of the goat is the bounty of God" and "The wrath of the lion is the wisdom of God."

Blake's vision has the scope of religion and yet burns with the intensity of a unique genius, making the outpouring of Transcendentalism in New England during the next century seem pale by comparison. Emerson, in "Brahma," was copping a few well-worn lines from the *Bhagavad Gita* when he wrote:

> If the red slayer think he slays,
>   Or if the slain think he is slain,
> They know not well the subtle ways
>   I keep, and pass, and turn again.
>
> Far or forgot to me is near;
>   Shadow and sunlight are the same;
> The vanished gods to me appear;
>   And one to me are shame and fame.

New England Yankees couldn't understand it. They thought Emerson was talking about himself. The word "Brahmin" became a synonym for aristocratic aloofness.

Yet the foundations were being laid for another generation and a poet who was as distinctively American as Blake was English. In Walt Whitman, the god of a million aspects becomes the transcendence of all being. Multiplicity as God. And Whitman was talking unabashedly about himself—sounding that barbaric yawp which echoes today in Allen Ginsberg.

Rock during the sixties had no counterpart to Walt Whitman. It had nothing, at least on the level of words, to match Whitman's expansive love, his exuberance, his diversity. Midwestern farmer, Brooklyn hod carrier, fugitive slave, cabinet maker, Southern lady, soldier, sailor, blacksmith, lover—he delighted in every role.

Dylan came closest to matching Whitman's diversity. But the world which Whitman had embraced so robustly a hundred years before seemed in the fifties and sixties to be poisoned. The roles of work which Whitman delighted in had been replaced by key-punch operator, Vice-President in charge of Personnel, and Turner-of-screw-in-Detroit-Auto-Factory. The only color left was the color of sickness and the amusement park roles of con artists, shills and geeks, hobos, hustlers, meth-heads and transvestites who parodied the society overhead.

It was equally clear that Whitman's portion of health could not be usurped forever. Negativity just didn't pull you through. The Underground was wallowing.

New Morning was a move toward recovering the vision of America that had been lost. Its qualified optimism could come honestly only from an artist who had paid his dues in despair and hate, and whose earlier obsession with sickness was, for him—as it was for Lenny Bruce—the truest possible expression of health.

Father of Night

BOB DYLAN

Father of night, Father of day,
Father, Who taketh the darkness away;
Father, Who teacheth the bird to fly,
Builder of rainbows up in the sky;
Father of loneliness and pain,
Father of love and Father of rain.

Father of day, Father of night,
Father of black, Father of white;
Father, Who build the mountain so high,
Who shapeth the cloud up in the sky;
Father of time, and Father of dreams,
Father, Who turneth the rivers and the streams.

Father of grain, Father of wheat,
Father of cold and Father of heat;
Father of air and Father of trees
Who dwells in our hearts and our memories.
Father of minutes, Father of days;
Father of Whom we most solemnly praise.

Song of Myself (22)

WALT WHITMAN

Sea of stretch'd ground-swells,
Sea breathing broad and convulsive breaths,
Sea of the brine of life and of unshovell'd yet always-ready
    graves,
Howler and scooper of storms, capricious and dainty sea,
I am integral with you, I too am of one phase and of all
    phases.

Partaker of influx and efflux I, extoller of hate and
    conciliation,
Extoller of amies and those that sleep in each others' arms,

I am he attesting sympathy,
(Shall I make my list of things in the house and skip the house
                     that supports them?)

I am not the poet of goodness only, I do not decline to be the
    poet of wickedness also.

"Woodstock," by Joni Mitchell,
    recorded on *Ladies of the Canyon,* 1970
"To the Garden the World," by Walt Whitman (1819–1892),
    from *Children of Adam,* 1860

Maybe he didn't actually have a guitar, and possibly he wasn't walking along the road to Woodstock; but he was part of the something turning. Whitman was there.

In 1860 he was talking about

    Potent mates, daughters, sons preluding
    The love, the life of their bodies, meaning and being

ascending anew to the garden, the world; Whitman following along, leading. A child of God. A father.

Eden—the whole notion of a lost paradise—haunts all the great religions of the West. The Greek genesis told of four ages; people of gold, giving way to silver, giving way to brass and then iron. For the Indians of the southwestern United States it was an age of gold, descending to silver, to copper and then to a mixed mineral. And everywhere, this degeneration from pristine wisdom is likened to the child's innocence giving way to adult cynicism.

> We are stardust
> We are golden
> And we've got to get ourselves
> Back to the garden

The sense of cycle, of "resurrection," of being a "cog in something turning," is basic to Joni Mitchell's song and Walt Whitman's poem. The difference is one of tense. What is an imperative for the future in "Woodstock" is happening *now* for Whitman. In "To the Garden the World" the cycle is not a Ferris wheel where a generation must wait its turn, but a continuous renewal; not a time of year or even a "time of man," not even a generation, but a perpetual regeneration.

Woodstock

JONI MITCHELL

I came upon a child of God
He was walking along the road
And I asked him, where are you going
And this he told me
I'm going on down to Yasgurs' farm
I'm going to join in a rock 'n' roll band
I'm going to camp out on the land
And then try an' get my soul free

We are stardust
We are golden
And we've got to get ourselves
Back to the garden

Then can I walk beside you
I have come here to lose the smog
And I feel to be a cog in something turning
Well maybe it is just the time of year
Or maybe it's the time of man
I don't know who I am
But you know life is for learning
We are stardust
We are golden
And we've got to get ourselves
Back to the garden

By the time we got to Woodstock
We were half a million strong
And everywhere there was song and celebration
And I dreamed I saw the bombers
Riding shotgun in the sky
And they were turning into butterflies
Above our nation
We are stardust (billion-year-old carbon)
We are golden (caught in the devil's bargain)
And we've got to get ourselves
Back to the garden

To the Garden the World

WALT WHITMAN

To the garden the world anew ascending,
Potent mates, daughters, sons, preluding,
The love, the life of their bodies, meaning and being,
Curious here behold my resurrection after slumber,

The revolving cycles in their wide sweep having brought me
    again,
Amorous, mature, all beautiful to me, all wondrous,
My limbs and the quivering fire that ever plays through them,
    for reasons, most wondrous,
Existing I peer and penetrate still,
Content with the present, content with the past,
By my side or back of me Eve following,
Or in front, and I following her just the same.

"We Can Be Together," by Paul Kantner,
    recorded on The Jefferson Airplane's *Volunteers*, 1970
Song of Myself (24), by Walt Whitman (1819–1892),
    from 1855 edition of *Song of Myself*

Here is a manifesto of the self striving to be plural and a manifesto
for the plural self trying to be singular. They meet somewhere in
their paradoxes.

Whitman's proclamation, "Unscrew the locks from the doors!"
celebrates not only the anarchy of his own fleshy appetites but
also his unity with all mankind. And Paul Kantner's "Tear down
the walls" aims at unifying the very forces of "chaos and anarchy."

Despite the declarative tone of Whitman's poem, his lines stay
fluid, owing partly to the device of repeating key words to link
ideas rhythmically. This stylistic grace is at one with the philosophical pulse of the poem, from within to without, from without
to within—"surging . . . through me to the current and index"—
Whitman as a bewhiskered bivalve, taking in and expelling the
cosmos.

Quite a different exuberance is projected by the Airplane song,
with its flat vocals and fudged transitions suggesting a practice
drill by a citizens' militia. The stridence is the plain brown
wrapper for Revolution-Marketed-as-Teen-Fantasy: a harmless
plastic bomb for the old folks, at $4.98 a throw.

We Can Be Together

PAUL KANTNER

We can be together
Ah you and me
We should be together

We are all outlaws in the eyes of America
In order to survive we steal cheat lie forge fred hide and deal
We are obscene lawless hideous dangerous dirty violent and
    young

But we should be together
Come on all you people standing around
Our life's too fine to let it die and
We can be together

All your private property is
Target for your enemy
And your enemy is
We

We are forces of chaos and anarchy
Everything they say we are we are
And we are very
Proud of ourselves

Up against the wall
Up against the wall fred
Tear down the walls
Tear down the walls

Come on now together
Get it on together
Everybody together

We should be together
We should be together my friends
We can be together
We will be

We must begin here and now
A new continent of earth and fire
Tear down the walls
Come on now gettin higher and higher
Tear down the walls
Tear down the walls
Tear down the walls
Won't you try

Song of Myself (24)

WALT WHITMAN

Walt Whitman, an American, one of the roughs, a kosmos,
Disorderly, fleshy and sensual . . . . eating drinking
    and breeding,
No sentimentalist . . . . no stander above men and women
    or apart from them . . . no more modest than immodest.

Unscrew the locks from the doors!
Unscrew the doors themselves from their jambs!

Whoever degrades another degrades me . . . . and
    whatever is done or said returns at last to me,
And whatever I do or say I also return.
Through me the afflatus surging and surging . . . . through
    me the current and index.

I speak the password primeval . . . . I give the sign of
    democracy;
By God! I will accept nothing which all cannot have their
    counterpart of on the same terms.

"Wooden Ships," by David Crosby, Paul Kantner, Stephen Stills, recorded on *Crosby, Stills and Nash*, 1969
"Asia's Song," by Percy Bysshe Shelley (1792–1822), from *Prometheus Unbound*, II, 5, 1819

"Wooden Ships," by David Crosby and Stephen Sills, may be listened to as a science fiction freakout. This seems to be the fervent hope of The Jefferson Airplane, who in cutting its own version for *Volunteers* evidently decided that Crosby and Stills, like the Delphic Oracle, had left certain details a trifle fuzzy; so The Airplane prefaced its own version with an explanation of how the "silver people on the shoreline" were really silver-suited people scrounging uncontaminated food; and how—in case you weren't hip—the wood of the ships was proof against radioactivity; and the people on the ship were free happy crazy beautiful freaks.

All of which serves to point out that as propaganda *cum* science fiction, "Wooden Ships" is not only trash, it is painfully close to the ads for bomb shelters with color phones and television.

But the song suffers needlessly from this approach, which is at bottom, I think, a brutalized approach. Its subject is difficult and painful enough, whether you listen to it as science fantasy or as a metaphor for the trip we are all taking to some extent right now. The song itself, both the original on *Crosby, Stills and Nash* and the jointly revised form presented here, is deserving of a more innocent and at the same time less literal response.

Consider "Asia's Song" by Shelley. The enchanted boat is the soul, carried forward by song, but it is also "the boat of my desire." The metaphor is left to grow within the reader's mind, its delicacy conveyed by Shelley's lines, which flow downstream looping, softly bumping; an impossibly light craft winding its way down to "a sea profound, of ever-spreading sound."

The shore is left behind, the hazards of Infancy and Age are safely avoided. Driven without a course, piloted by the instinct of sweet music, the boat drifts to "realms where the air we breathe is love."

"Wooden Ships"—left to the strengths of its own haunting melody and lyrics—moves not so differently. Though the mood of the Crosby, Kantner and Stills version is edged with melancholy, with the knowledge of those people left on the shore, still the movement is toward sharing and a new freedom. And if it lacks the emotional dynamism of a song written in an opposite vein to show the hijacking of a soul—Bernie Taupin's "Take Me to the Pilot"—it nevertheless allows the metaphor some of the same room to move.

The silver people. Yes, they are wearing silver suits, but they are *silver people*.

The berries, on the other hand. Consider the effect on the song if that particular detail were left out.

The wood—not just somehow radiation-proof, but an antidote to the plasticity of a barren culture. An escape to some kind of authentic alternative.

Once when the city of Athens was about to be besieged by its enemies, the Oracle at Delphi advised the Athenians to take refuge behind "wooden walls." Wooden ships proved to be their salvation in the Battle of Salamis.

If the Athenians had taken the Oracle's advice literally, they would have perished. But their response was as creative as it was realistic—as creative as some of the efforts of people today, young and old, to set out and create a new and authentic culture.

Wooden Ships

DAVID CROSBY, PAUL KANTNER, STEPHEN STILLS

(UPS) EARTH JULY 1975
Black sails knifing through the pitchblende night
Away from the radioactive landmass madness
From the silver-suited people searching out
Uncontaminated food and shelter on the shores
No glowing metal on our ship of wood only
Free happy crazy people naked in the universe
WE SPEAK EARTH TALK
GO RIDE THE MUSIC

If you smile at me you know I will understand
'Cause that is something everybody does
In the same language
I can see by your coat my friend that you're from the other
side
There's just one thing I got to know
Can you tell me please who won
You must try some of my purple berries
I been eating them for six or seven weeks now
Haven't got sick once
Probably keep us both alive

Wooden ships on the water very free and easy
Easy you know the way it's supposed to be
Silver people on the shoreline leave us be
Very free and easy

Sail away where the mornin' sun goes high
Sail away where the wind blows sweet and young birds fly
Take a sister by her hand
Lead her far from this barren land

Horror grips us as we watch you die
All we can do is echo your anguished cry and
Stare as all your human feelings die
We are leaving
You don't need us

Go and take a sister by her hand
Lead her far from this foreign land
Somewhere where we might laugh again
We are leaving
You don't need us

Asia's Song

PERCY BYSSHE SHELLEY

My Soul is an enchanted boat,
　　Which, like a sleeping swan, doth float
Upon the silver waves of thy sweet singing;
　　And thine doth like an angel sit
　　Beside a helm conducting it,
Whilst all the winds with melody are ringing.
　　It seems to float ever, for ever,
　　Upon that many-winding river,
　　Between mountains, woods, abysses,
　　A paradise of wildernesses!
Till, like one in slumber bound,
Borne to the ocean, I float down, around,
Into a sea profound, of ever-spreading sound:

　　Meanwhile thy spirit lifts its pinions
　　In music's most serene dominions;
Catching the winds that fan that happy heaven.
　　And we sail on, away, afar,
　　Without a course, without a star,
But, by the instinct of sweet music driven;
　　Till through Elysian garden islets
　　By thee, most beautiful of pilots,
　　Where never mortal pinnace glided,
　　The boat of my desire is guided:
Realms where the air we breathe is love,
Which in the winds and on the waves doth move,
Harmonizing this earth with what we feel above.

　　We have passed Age's icy caves,
　　And Manhood's dark and tossing waves,
And Youth's smooth ocean, smiling to betray:
　　Beyond the glassy gulfs we flee
　　Of shadow-peopled Infancy,
Through Death and Birth, to a diviner day;
　　A paradise of vaulted bowers,

Lit by downward-gazing flowers,
  And watery paths that wind between
  Wildernesses calm and green,
Peopled by shapes too bright to see,
And rest, having beheld; somewhat like thee;
Which walk upon the sea, and chant melodiously!

"New Morning," by Bob Dylan,
  from *New Morning*, 1970
"Song," from Robert Browning (1812–1889),
  from *Pippa Passes*, 1841

These two celebrations of the morning, the one by nineteenth-century poet Robert Browning and the other by Bob Dylan, are distinguished from others by their *transcendence*. Jackie Washington's "Morning Song" and Joni Mitchell's "Chelsea Morning," for instance, use morning as background for the Self. Even Paul Simon's "The 59th Street Bridge Song (Feelin' Groovy)" celebrates a mood of the early morning, and not the morning itself. But Browning's "Song" and Dylan's "New Morning" leave the Self behind.

Both are qualified prayers, in their exaltation of all things living—the lark, the rabbit, the snail—and all things inanimate—the dew, the sun—even, in Browning's poem, the thorn; in Dylan's song, even the automobile. An affirmation of All Being which transcends the Self.

Yet both are qualified in time, with ironic effect. Browning's God is in his heaven at this best of all hours, but the announcement carries the implication that this is not always so, that at less groovy times He may be off-duty.

In "New Morning," the irony is as subtle. The pastoral setting and the "automobile comin' into style" tend to push the calendar back fifty or sixty years to the country idyll that *was*, the morning we might experience if only we could drive back in our flivvers to where the road forked, and one sign said HAPPINESS and the other said PROGRESS. And perhaps we can, Dylan seems to say. Maybe it is not too late—if not for a cabin in Utah, then for a personal reordering of those highway signs, a reshaping of the old myths.

Whatever the ironic qualifications, both poets are passionately optimistic. Whatever page is showing in Dylan's calendar, his exuberance, his engaging stroll with *you* while pointing to the immediacy of experience unrolling under shoesoles and sounded against human eardrums, all speak insistently in the present. Browning, with the childlike purity of his images, his ejaculatory *Hey man, dig!* rhythm, sounds the same clarion advertisement for the moment. If anything, that edge of irony underlying both lends force to their optimism.

Dylan, by turning the clock back, compresses a knowledge of all the ugliness of the past few decades—his own vision of hell, along with Joni Mitchell's "Big Yellow Taxi" and Tom Paxton's "Whose Garden Was This?"—compresses it all, and takes us back to a time before they paved Desolation Row, with the hope of saving something old by making it new.

New Morning

BOB DYLAN

Can't you hear that rooster crowin'?
Rabbit runnin' down across the road
Underneath the bridge where the water flowed through.
So happy just to see you smile, underneath the sky of blue
On this new morning, new morning,
On this new morning, with you.

Can't you hear that motor turnin'?
Automobile comin' into style,
Comin' down the road for a country mile or two.
So happy just to see you smile, underneath this sky of blue
On this new morning, new morning,
On this new morning, with you.

The night passed away so quickly;
It always does when you're with me.
Can't you feel that sun a-shinin'?
Groundhog runnin' by the country stream,
This must be the day that all of my dreams come true.
So happy just to be alive underneath this sky of blue
On this new morning, new morning,
On this new morning, with you.

So happy just to be alive, underneath this sky of blue
On this new morning, new morning,
On this new morning with you.

New morning,
New morning.

Song

ROBERT BROWNING

The year's at the spring
And day's at the morn;
Morning's at seven;
The hill-side's dew-pearled;
The lark's on the wing;
The snail's on the thorn:
God's in his heaven—
All's right with the world!

PROSE gets in the way sometimes. . . .
Here are some poems and songs brought together without comment.

Dawn Is a Feeling

MIKE PINDER

Dawn is a feeling, a beautiful ceiling
The smell of grass just makes you pass
Into a dream.

You're here today, no future fears
This day will last one thousand years
If you want it to.

"Dawn Is a Feeling," by Mike Pinder. Used by permission of Kenwood Music, Inc. Recorded by The Moody Blues on *Days of Future Passed,* 1968.

You look around, things astound you
So breathe in deep, you're not asleep
Open your mind.

You're here today, no future fears
This day will last one thousand years
If you want it to.

You understand that all over this land there's a feeling
In minds far and near things are becoming clear with a
    meaning
Down at your knowing pleasures start flowing
It's true life flies faster than eyes could ever see

You're here today, no future fears
This day will last a thousand years
If you want it to.

The Dream (Part 1)

GEORGE GORDON, LORD BYRON (1789–1824)

Our life is two-fold: Sleep hath its own world,
A boundary between the things misnamed
Death and existence: Sleep hath its own world,
And a wide realm of wild reality.
And dreams in their development have breath,
And tears, and tortures, and the touch of joy;
They leave a weight upon our waking thoughts,
They take a weight from off our waking toils,
They do divide our being; they become
A portion of ourselves as of our time,
And look like heralds of eternity;
They pass like spirits of the past,—they speak
Like Sibyls of the future: they have power—
The tyranny of pleasure and of pain;

(Written in 1816)

They make us what we were not—what they will,
And shake us with the vision that's gone by,
The dread of vanish'd shadows—Are they so?
Is not the past all shadow?—What are they?
Creations of the mind?—The mind can make
Substance, and people planets of its own
With beings brighter than have been, and give
A breath to forms which can outlive all flesh.
I would recall a vision which I dream'd
Perchance in sleep—for in itself a thought,
A slumbering thought, is capable of years,
And curdles a long life into one hour.

Chelsea Morning

JONI MITCHELL

Woke up, it was Chelsea morning
And the first thing that I heard
Was song outside my window
And the traffic wrote the words.
It came ringing up like Christmas bells
And rapping up like pipes and drums.

Oh, won't you stay? We'll put on the day
And we'll wear it till the night comes.

Woke up, it was a Chelsea morning
And the first thing that I saw
Was the sun through yellow curtains
And a rainbow on my wall,
Red, green and gold to welcome you,
Crimson crystal beads to beckon.

Oh, won't you stay and we'll put on the day?
There's a sun show every second.

Now the curtain opens on a portrait of today
And the streets are paved with passers by
And pigeons fly and papers lie
Waiting to blow away.

Woke up, it was Chelsea morning
And the first thing that I knew
There was milk and toast and honey
And a bowl of oranges, too,
And the light poured in like butterscotch
And stuck to all my senses.

Oh, won't you stay? We'll put on the day
And we'll talk in present tenses.

When the curtain closes
And the rainbow runs away,
I will bring you incense owls at night
By candlelight, by jewel-light
If only you will stay.

Pretty baby, won't you
Wake up. It's a Chelsea morning.

The Morning Watch

HENRY VAUGHAN (1621–1695)

O Joyes! Infinite sweetness! with what flowres,
And shoots of glory, my soul breakes, and buds!
    All the long houres
    Of night, and Rest
    Through the still shrouds
    Of sleep, and Clouds,

From *The Silex Scintillans*, 1650

120

This Dew fell on my Breast;
    O how it Blouds,
And Spirits all my Earth! heark! In what Rings,
And Hymning Circulations the quick world
        Awakes, and sings;
        The rising winds,
        And falling springs,
        Birds, beasts, all things
    Adore him in their kinds.
        Thus all is hurl'd
In sacred Hymnes, and Order, The great Chime
And Symphony of nature. Prayer is
        The world in tune,
        A spirit-voyce,
        And recall joyes
    Whose Eccho is heav'ns blisse.
        O let me climbe
When I lye down! The pious soul by night
Is like a clouded starre, whose beames though sed
        To shed their light
        Under some Cloud
        Yet are above,
        And shine, and move
    Beyond that mistie shrowd.
        So in my Bed
That Curtain'd grave, though sleep, like ashes, hide
My lamp, and life, both shall in thee abide.

Cactus Tree

JONI MITCHELL

There's a man who's been out sailing
In a decade full of dreams
And he takes her to a schooner
And he treats her like a queen,

"Cactus Tree," words and music by Joni Mitchell, © 1968. Reprinted by permission of the publishers, Siquomb Publishing Corp. Recorded on *Joni Mitchell*, 1968.

Bearing beads from California
With their amber stones and green
He has called her from the harbor;
He has kissed her with his freedom;
He has heard her off to starboard
In the breaking and the
Breathing of the water weeds,
While she's so busy being free.

There's a man who's climbed a mountain
And he's calling out her name
And he hopes her heart can hear
Three thousand miles; he calls again.
He can think her there beside him;
He can miss her just the same.
He has missed her in the forest
While he showed her all the flowers
And the branches sang the chorus
As he climbed the scaley towers
Of a forest tree,
While she was somewhere being free.

There's a man who's sent a letter
And he's waiting for reply;
He has asked her of her travels
Since the day they said goodbye.
He writes, "Wish you were beside me;
We can make it if we try."
He has seen her at the office
With her name on all his papers;
Thru the sharing of the profits
He will find it hard to shake
Her from his memory,
And she's so busy being free.

There's a lady in the city
And she thinks she loves them all.
There's the one who's thinking of her;
There's the one who sometimes calls;

There's the one who writes her letters
With his facts and figures scrawl.
She has brought them to her senses;
They have laughed inside her laughter.
Now she rallies her defenses
For she fears that one will ask her
For eternity.
And she's so busy being free.

There's a man who sends her medals;
He is bleeding from the war.
There's a jouster and a jester
And a man who owns a store.
There's a drummer and a dreamer
And you know there may be more.
She will love them when she sees them;
They will lose her if they follow.
And she only means to please them
And her heart is full and hollow
Like a cactus tree,
While she's so busy being free.

Unthrifty Loveliness (Sonnet IV)

WILLIAM SHAKESPEARE (1564–1616)

Unthrifty loveliness, why dost thou spend
Upon thyself thy beauty's legacy?
Nature's bequest gives nothing, but doth lend,
And, being frank, she lends to those are free.
Then, bounteous niggard, why dost thou abuse
The bounteous largess given thee to give?
Profitless usurer, why dost thou use
So great a sum of sums, yet canst not live?
For, having traffic with thyself alone,
Thou of thyself thy sweet self dost deceive.
Then how, when nature calls thee to be gone,

What acceptable audit canst thou leave?
    Thy unus'd beauty must be tomb'd with thee,
    Which, used, lives th' executor to be.

Gypsy Eyes

JIMI HENDRIX

Way up in my tree I'm sitting by my fire
Wond'rin' where in this world might you be.
And knowing all the time you still are roamin' the countryside.
Do you still think about me?

Well, I realize that I've been hypnotized
I love you, Gypsy Eyes . . . I love you, Gypsy Eyes
I love you, Gypsy Eyes . . . I love you, Gypsy Eyes.

Well, I walk right on up to your rebel roadside
The one that rambles on for a million miles
Well, I walk down this road
Searching for your love and-uh my soul too
And when I find you, I ain't gonna let go.

I remember the first time I saw you
The tears in your eyes look like they was try'n to say
"Oh, little boy, you know I could love you
But first, I must make my getaway,
Two strange men fighting to the death over me today. . . .
I'll try to meet you by the old highway."

Well, I realize that I've been hypnotized
I love you, Gypsy Eyes . . . I love you, Gypsy Eyes
I love you, Gypsy Eyes . . . I love you, Gypsy Eyes.

I've been searching so long,
My feet, they painfully leave the battle
Down against the road my weary knees take their place
Off to the side I fall
But I hear a sweet call
My Gypsy Eyes has found me and I've been saved
Lord, I've been saved
That's why I love you
Lord knows, I love you.

Sweet-and-Twenty

WILLIAM SHAKESPEARE (1564–1616)

O Mistress mine, where are you roaming?
  O, stay and hear! your true love's coming,
  That can sing both high and low:
Trip no further, pretty sweeting;
Journeys end in lovers meeting,
  Every wise man's son doth know.
  What is love? 'tis not hereafter;
  Present mirth had present laughter;
  What's to come is still unsure:
  In delay there lies no plenty;
  Then come kiss me, sweet-and-twenty!
    Youth's a stuff will not endure.

From *Twelfth Night*, ca. 1602.

I Think I Understand

JONI MITCHELL

Daylight falls upon the path, the forest falls behind
Today I am not prey to dark uncertainty
The shadow trembles in its wrath, I've robbed its
    blackness blind
And tasted sunlight as my fear came clear to me

I think I understand
Fear is like a wilderland
Stepping stones on sinking sand

Now the way leads to the hills, above the steeple's chime
Below me sleepy rooftops round the harbor
It's there I'll take my thirsty fill of friendship over wine
Forgetting fear but never disregarding her

Oh, I think I understand
Fear is like a wilderland
Stepping stones on sinking sand

Sometimes voices in the night will call me back again
Back along the pathway of a troubled mind
When forests rise to block the light that keeps a traveler sane
I'll challenge them with flashes from a brighter time

Oh, I think I understand
Fear is like a wilderland
Stepping stones on sinking sand

Our Journey Had Advanced

EMILY DICKINSON (1830–1886)

Our journey had advanced;
Our feet were almost come
To that odd fork in Being's road,
Eternity by term.

Our pace took sudden awe,
Our feet reluctant led.
Before were cities, but between,
The forest of the dead.

Retreat was out of hope,—
Behind, a sealed route,
Eternity's white flag before,
And God at every gate.

Strawberry Fields Forever

JOHN LENNON and PAUL McCARTNEY

Let me take you down,
'cos I'm going to Strawberry Fields.
Nothing is real
and nothing to get hungabout.
Strawberry Fields forever.
Living is easy with eyes closed
Misunderstanding all you see.
It's getting hard to be someone.
But it all works out,

"Our Journey Had Advanced," by Emily Dickinson. Reprinted by permission of the publishers and the Trustees of Amherst College from Thomas H. Johnson, Editor, *The Poems of Emily Dickinson*, Cambridge, Mass.: The Belknap Press of Harvard University Press, Copyright, 1951, 1955, by The President and Fellows of Harvard College. From *Poems*, 1891.

"Strawberry Fields Forever," by John Lennon and Paul McCartney. Reprinted from *The Beatles Illustrated Lyrics* by permission of Delacorte Press/A Seymour Lawrence Book. Recorded on The Beatles' *Magical Mystery Tour*, 1967.

it doesn't matter much to me.
Let me take you down,
'cos I'm going to Strawberry Fields.
Nothing is real
and nothing to get hungabout.
Strawberry Fields forever.
No one I think is in my tree,
I mean it must be high or low.
That is you can't you know tune in.
But it's all right.
That is I think it's not too bad.
Let me take you down,
'cos I'm going to Strawberry Fields.
Nothing is real
and nothing to get hungabout.
Strawberry Fields forever.
Always, no sometimes, think it's me,
but you know I know when it's a dream.
I think I know I mean a "Yes."
But it's all wrong.
That is I think I disagree.
Let me take you down,
'cos I'm going to Strawberry Fields.
Nothing is real
and nothing to get hungabout.
Strawberry Fields forever.
Strawberry Fields forever.

The Lotus Eaters

ALFRED, LORD TENNYSON (1809–1892)

(Choric Songs 3 and 4)

Lo! in the middle of the wood,
The folded leaf is wooed from out the bud
With winds upon the branch, and there
Grows green and broad, and takes no care,
Sun-steeped at noon, and in the moon
Nightly dew-fed; and turning yellow
Falls, and floats adown the air.
Lo! sweetened with the sunner light,
The full-juiced apple, waxing over-mellow,
Drops in a silent autumn night.
All its allotted length of days
The flower ripens in its place,
Ripens and fades, and falls, and hath no toil,
Fast-rooted in the fruitful soil.

Hateful is the dark blue sky,
Vaulted o'er the dark blue sea.
Death is the end of life; ah, why
Should life all labor be?
Let us alone. Time driveth onward fast,
And in a little while our lips are dumb.
Let us alone. What is it that will last?
All things are taken from us, and become
Portions and parcels of the dreadful past.
Let us alone. What pleasure can we have
To war with evil? Is there any peace
In ever climbing up the climbing wave?
All things have rest, and ripen toward the grave
In silence—ripen, fall, and cease:
Give us long rest or death, dark death, or dreamful ease.

From *Poems,* 1833.

She Wandered Through the Garden Fence

KEITH REID

She wandered through the garden fence
And said, "I've bought at great expense
A potion guaranteed to bring
Relief from all your suffering."
Although I said, "You don't exist,"
She grasped me firmly by the wrist
And threw me down upon my back
And strapped me to her torture rack.
And without further argument
I found my mind was also bent
Upon a course so devious
It only made my torment worse.

She said, "I see you cannot speak.
Is it your voice that is too weak?
Is it your tongue that is to blame?
Maybe you cannot speak for shame.
Or has your brain been idle too,
And now it will not think for you?
I hastened to make my reply
But found that I could only lie.
And like a fool I believed myself
And thought I was somebody else
But she could see what I was then
And left me on my own again.

The Mental Traveller

WILLIAM BLAKE (1757–1827)

I travel'd thro' a Land of Men,
A Land of Men & Women too,
And heard & saw such dreadful things
As cold Earth wanderers never knew.

For there the Babe is born in joy
That was begotten in dire woe;
Just as we Reap in joy the fruit
Which we in bitter tears did sow.

And if the Babe is born a Boy
He's given to a Woman Old,
Who nails him down upon a rock,
Catches his shrieks in cups of gold.

She binds iron thorns around his head,
She pierces both his hands & feet,
She cuts his heart out at his side
To make it feel both cold & heat.

Her fingers number every Nerve.
Just as a Miser counts his gold;
She lives upon his shrieks & cries,
And she grows young as he grows old.

Till he becomes a bleeding youth,
And she becomes a Virgin bright;
Then he rends up his Manacles
And binds her down for his delight.

He plants himself in all her Nerves,
Just as a Husbandman his mould;
And she becomes his dwelling place
And Garden fruitful seventy fold.

From the Pickering Manuscript, 1803

An aged Shadow, soon he faces,
Wand'ring round an Earthly Cot,
Full filled all with gems & gold
Which he by industry had got.

And these are the gems of the Human Soul,
The rubies & pearls of a lovesick eye,
The countless gold of the akeing heart,
The martyr's groan & the lover's sigh.

They are his meat, they are his drink;
He feeds the Beggar & the Poor
And the wayfaring Traveller:
For ever open is his door.

His grief is their eternal joy;
They make the roofs & walls to ring;
Till from the fire on the hearth
A little Female Babe does spring.

And she is all of solid fire
And gems & gold, that none his hand
Dares stretch to touch her Baby form,
Or wrap her in his swaddling-band.

But She comes to the Man she loves,
If young or old, or rich or poor;
They soon drive out the aged Host,
A Beggar at another's door.

He wanders weeping far away,
Untill some other take him in;
Oft blind & age-bent, sore distrest,
Untill he can a Maiden win.

And to allay his freezing Age
The Poor Man takes her in his arms;
The Cottage fades before his sight,
The Garden & its lovely Charms.

The Guests are scatter'd thro' the land,
For the Eye altering alters all;
The Senses roll themselves in fear,
And the flat Earth becomes a Ball;

The stars, sun, Moon, all shrink away,
A desart vast without a bound,
And nothing left to eat or drink,
And a dark desart all around.

The honey of her Infant lips,
The bread & wine of her sweet smile,
The wild game of her roving Eye,
Does him to Infancy beguile;

For as he eats & drinks he grows
Younger & younger every day;
And on the desart wild they both
Wander in terror & dismay.

Like the wild Stag she flees away,
Her fear plants many a thicket wild;
While he pursues her night & day,
By various arts of Love beguil'd,

By various arts of Love & Hate,
Till the wide desart planted o'er
With Labyrinths of wayward Love,
Where roam the Lion, Wolf & Boar,

Till he becomes a wayward Babe,
And she a weeping Woman Old.
Then many a Lover wanders here;
The Sun & Stars are nearer roll'd.

The trees bring forth sweet Extacy
To all who in the desart roam;
Till many a City there is Built,
And many a pleasant Shepherd's home.

But when they find the frowning Babe,
Terror strikes thro' the region wide:
They cry "The Babe! the Babe is Born!"
And flee away on Every side.

For who dare touch the frowning form,
His arm is wither'd to its root;
Lions, Boars, Wolves, all howling flee,
And every Tree does shed its fruit.

And none can touch that frowning form,
Except it be a Woman Old;
She nails him down upon the Rock,
And all is done as I have told.

FINAL NOTES

OMITTED from this book were all those songs which take their lyrics verbatim from traditional poems. But to the reader interested in pursuing these, it would be worthwhile listening to Donovan's treatment of "Under the Greenwood Tree"; Pete Seeger's "Ariel's Song," adapted from *The Tempest;* and an unusual album by Principal Edwards Magic Theatre which incorporates Shakespeare's "Third Sonnet to Sundry Notes of Music." (PEMT is an English group, virtually unknown, but doing some exciting things in rock theatre.) In addition to these, Phil Ochs has arranged Poe's "The Bells," Dave van Ronk sings Yeats' "The Song of the Wandering Aengus," and on their first album The Fugs do two poems by Blake, "Ah! Sunflower Weary of Time" and "How Sweet I Roam'd from Field to Field." Hamlet, of course, soliloquizes in "What a Piece of Work Is Man," used in *Hair.*

Three books on rock which I continue to find useful are:

Jonathan Eisen's *The Age of Rock.* New York: Vintage Books (Random House), 1969. (Collected essays; generally tighter than Eisen's second book)

Richard Goldstein's *The Poetry of Rock.* New York: Bantam Books, 1969. (Lyrics)

Lillian Roxon's *Rock Encyclopedia*. New York: Grosset & Dunlap, 1969. (The best and only rock encyclopedia)

For newcomers to rock, Paul Williams' *Outlaw Blues* is good fun and preferable to the histories (New York: E. P. Dutton & Co., Inc., 1969). All four of the above are available in paperbound editions.

For someone wanting to start a home library of rock albums and not wanting to spend a fortune, four records—while not offering anything like balance—would at least give a sampling of good lyrics. All are several years old.

Bob Dylan's *Bringing It All Back Home*
The Beatles' *Sergeant Pepper's Lonely Hearts Club Band*
Songs of Leonard Cohen
Joni Mitchell

If they aren't to be found in your local public library, become irate.

INDEX OF TITLES, AUTHORS AND PERFORMERS

"The Abyss," 29
"Albatross," 36, 37
Arnold, Matthew, 35
"Asia's Song," 107, 110–11

"Bad Moon Rising," 85
Baudelaire, Charles, 28–30
The Beatles, 42, 70, 71, 73, 75, 127
"Bhagavad Gita," 98
"Bishop Cody's Last Request," 54, 55–57
"The Bishop Orders His Tomb at St. Praxed's Church," 57
Blaikley, Howard, 18, 20
Blake, William, 76, 77, 78, 131
Browning, Robert, 54, 55, 57–60, 111, 114
"buffalo bill's," 76
Byron, Lord, 118–19

"Cactus Tree," 121–23
"Casey Jones," 52
"Chelsea Morning," 119–20
Clapton, Eric, and Sharp, Martin, 9, 10, 11

Cohen, Leonard, 14–16, 32–34, 88
Collins, Judy, 36
"The Continuing Story of Bungalow Bill," 75
Cream, 10, 11
Creedence Clearwater Revival, 85
Crosby, David, Paul Kantner, and Stephen Stills, 107
Crosby, Stills and Nash, 107
Crosby, Stills, Nash and Young, 28
cummings, e. e., 74, 76

"The Dawn," 73
"Dawn Is a Feeling," 117–18
"The Death of Kings," 93
Dickinson, Emily, 127
"A Dirge," 86
"Dover Beach," 32, 35–36
"The Dream (Part 1)," 118–19
Dylan, Bob, 66, 67, 68–69, 98, 99, 100, 111–13

Emerson, Ralph Waldo, 99
"England in 1819," 70

"Father of Night," 98, 99, 100
Fogerty, John, 85–86
"The Fool on the Hill," 70, 71, 72–73
"Four and Twenty," 28, 29, 30
Fripp, Robert, and Peter Sinfield, 76, 78
"From the Underworld," 20

The Grateful Dead, 50, 51
"Gypsy Eyes," 124–25

Hendrix, Jimi, 124
The Herd, 18, 19
Homer, 9–11, 13
Hunter, Robert, 52

"In My Life," 42, 43
"I Think I Understand," 126

Jefferson Airplane, 104
John, Elton, 90, 91
"Joseph Mica," 53

Kantner, Paul, 104, 105–106, 107
King Crimson, 76, 77
"The King Must Die," 90, 91–92

Lamb, Charles, 42, 43–44
Leitch, Donovan, 79, 80
Lennon, John, and McCartney, Paul, 43, 72, 75, 127–28
"London," 78
"The Lotus Eaters (Choric Songs 3 and 4)," 129
Lowell, Amy, 36, 39–42

"Masters of War," 68
"The Mental Traveller," 131–34
Mitchell, Joni, 101, 102–103, 119, 121, 126
The Moody Blues, 117
"The Morning Watch," 120–21

"New Morning," 111–13

"The Observation," 79, 80
"The Old Familiar Faces," 43
"Orpheus and Eurydice," 21
"Our Journey Had Advanced," 127
Ovid, 21
Owen, Wilfred, 14–15, 18

"The Parable of the Old Men and the Young," 18
"Patterns," 39
Paxton, Tom, 3, 54–55
"Pictures of a City," 78
Pinder, Mike, 117
Procol Harum, 130

Reid, Keith, 130

"The Second Coming," 89
Shakespeare, William, 90, 91, 92, 123, 125
Shelley, Percy Bysshe, 66, 67, 70, 79, 80, 85, 86, 107, 110–11
"She Wandered Through the Garden Fence," 130
"The Sirens' Song," 13
"Song," 111, 113
"Song of Myself (22)," 98, 101
"Song of Myself (24)," 104, 106
Stills, Stephen, 28, 29, 30, 107
"Stories of the Street," 88
"Story of Issac," 16
"Strawberry Fields Forever," 127–28
"Suzanne," 32, 33–34
"Sweet-and-Twenty," 125

"Tales of Brave Ulysses," 11
Taupin, Bernie, 91
Tennyson, Lord Alfred, 129
"To the Garden the World," 101–104
"To the Reader," 30

"Unthrifty Loveliness (Sonnet IV)," 123–24

Vaughan, Henry, 120–21

"We Can Be Together," 105
Whitman, Walt, 97, 98, 99–100, 101–102, 103–104, 106
"Wooden Ships," 107, 108–109

"Woodstock," 101, 102–103

Yeats, William Butler, 32, 70, 73, 84, 86–87, 89–90
"Ye Hasten to the Grave!" 80

INDEX OF FIRST LINES

An old, mad, blind, despised, and dying king— 70

Bishop Cody's last request, 55

Buffalo Bill's, 76

Can't you hear that rooster crowin'? 112

Come you masters of war, 68

Concrete cold face cased in steel, 78

Dawn is a feeling, a beautiful ceiling, 117

Day after day, alone on a hill, 72

Daylight falls upon the path, the forest falls behind, 126

The door it opened slowly, 16

Driving that train, high on cocaine, 52

Father of night, Father of day, 100

Folly and error, avarice and vice, 30

Four and twenty years ago a-comin to this life, 30

Hey, Bungalow Bill, 75

I came upon a child of God, 102

I have had playmates, I have had companions, 43

I see a bad moon rising, 85

I travel'd thro' a Land of Men, 131

I walk down the garden paths, 39

I wander thro' each charter'd street, 78

I would be ignorant as the dawn, 73

Joseph Mica was good engineer, 53

The lady comes to the gate, 37

Let me take you down, 127

Let's talk of graves, of worms, and epitaphs. 93

Lo! in the middle of the wood, 129

My Soul is an enchanted boat, 110

No man's a jester playing Shakespeare, 91

O Joyes! Infinite sweetness! with what flowres, 120

O Mistress mine, where are you roaming? 125

On the sidewalk the people are bustling, 80

Our journey had advanced; 127

Our life is two-fold: Sleep has its own world, 118

Out of the land of shadows and darkness, 20

Pascal's abyss went with him,
  yawned in the air. 29
Rough wind, that moanest loud, 86
The sea is calm tonight, 35
Sea of stretch'd ground-swells, 101
She wandered through the garden
  fence, 130
So Abram rose, and clave the wood,
  and went, 18
The stories of the street are mine,
  88
Suzanne takes you down, 33
There are places I'll remember all my
  life, 43
There's a man who's been out sailing,
  121
They climbed the upward path,
  through absolute silence, 21
This way, oh turn your bows, 12

To the garden the world anew as-
  cending, 103
Turning and turning in the widening
  gyre, 89
Unthrifty loveliness, why dost thou
  spend, 123
(UPS) EARTH JULY 1975, 108
Vanity, saith the preacher, vanity! 57
Walt Whitman, an American, one of
  the roughs, a kosmos, 106
Way up in my tree I'm sitting by my
  fire, 124
We can be together, 105
Woke up, it was Chelsea morning,
  119
The year's at the spring, 113
Ye hasten to the grave! What seek
  ye there, 80
You thought the leaden winter, 11

ABOUT THE AUTHOR

DAVID MORSE was born in Vinita, Oklahoma, and spent most of his childhood in the suburbs of Washington, D.C. He attended Brown University briefly and was graduated from the University of Iowa. At 16 he worked as a photographer and political cartoonist for a weekly newspaper. After college Mr. Morse worked a year for *The New York Times*. He spent five years as a high-school English teacher, the last at the American School in London, but left there when he discovered that they were building the new school without windows. He is presently teaching at an alternative school.

David Morse lives in Norwich, Connecticut, with his wife, Ginny, and their sons, Scott and Bobby.